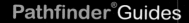
Pathfinder®Guides

Norfolk

Walks

Compiled by
Dennis and Jan Kelsall

Contents

At-a-glance

Walk	Page					
1 Horsey	10	Horsey Windpump	TG 457222	3¾ miles (6km)	N/a	1½ hrs
2 Binham Priory	12	Binham	TF 981399	4¼ miles (6.9km)	165ft (50m)	2 hrs
3 Oxborough and Gooderstone	14	Oxborough	TF 744014	5 miles (8km)	N/a	2 hrs
4 Hales Green from Loddon	16	Loddon	TM 362987	5¼ miles (8.4km)	165ft (50m)	2½ hrs
5 Marham Fen and the Nar Valley Way	18	Narborough	TF 750127	5½ miles (8.9km)	N/a	2½ hrs
6 Tyrrel's Wood and Shelton	20	Tyrrel's Wood	TM 205893	5½ miles (8.9km)	N/a	2½ hrs
7 Felbrigg Park and Metton	23	Felbrigg Hall	TG 194393	5¾ miles (9.3km)	180ft (55m)	2½ hrs
8 Langmere and the Devil's Punchbowl	26	East Wretham Heath	TL 912886	6 miles (9.7km)	N/a	2½ hrs
9 River Bure and Upton Marshes	29	South Walsham Broad	TG 372139	6 miles (9.7km)	N/a	2½ hrs
10 How Hill and Ludham	32	How Hill	TG 372189	6 miles (9.7km)	N/a	2½ hrs
11 The Buckenhams	36	Old Buckenham	TM 064915	6¼ miles (10km)	100ft (30m)	3 hrs
12 Hardley Cross	39	Chedgrave	TM 362993	6½ miles (10.5km)	80ft (25m)	3 hrs
13 Blickling and the River Bure	42	Buck's Common	TG 155290	6½ miles (10.5km)	195ft (60m)	3 hrs
14 Peddars Way - Fring and Sedgeford	44	Fring	TF 735348	7 miles (11.3km)	460ft (140m)	3½ hrs
15 Castle Acre and West Acre	47	Castle Acre	TF 817151	7 miles (11.3km)	280ft (85m)	3½ hrs
16 Boudica's Way - Shotesham & Saxlingham Nethergate	50	Shotesham	TM 246990	7 miles (11.3km)	245ft (75m)	3½ hrs
17 Thompson Common and the Pingos	53	Pingo Trail car park	TL 940965	7 miles (11.3km)	N/a	3½ hrs
18 Westwick Woods and the Weavers' Way	56	North Walsham	TG 275300	7 miles (11.3km)	215ft (65m)	3½ hrs
19 West Runton and Beacon Hill	59	East Runton	TG 200427	7¼ miles (11.7km)	575ft (175m)	3½ hrs
20 Wiveton Downs and Cley next the Sea	62	Wiveton Downs	TG 030422	7¾ miles (12.5km)	215ft (65m)	3½ hrs
21 The Burnhams	65	Burnham Market	TF 832421	7½ miles (12.1km)	230ft (70m)	3½ hrs
22 Denver Sluice - a three rivers walk	69	Fordham	TL 614995	8½ miles (13.7km)	N/a	4 hrs
23 Wells-next-the-Sea, Warham and Wighton	72	Wells-next-the-Sea	TF 915438	8½ miles (13.7km)	330ft (100m)	4 hrs
24 The Weavers' Way to The Berney Arms	76	Halvergate	TG 422069	9 miles (14.5km)	N/a	4 hrs
25 Reepham, Marriott's Way and Salle	79	Reepham	TG 101228	9¾ miles (15.7km)	245ft (75m)	4½ hrs
26 Weeting Castle and Grime's Graves	82	Santon Downham	TL 816877	10 miles (16.1km)	180ft (55m)	4½ hrs
27 Castle Rising and Roydon Common	85	Castle Rising	TF 666248	10½ miles (16.9km)	230ft (70m)	4½ hrs
28 Ringstead Downs and the Norfolk Coast	88	Holme next the Sea	TF 697438	11 miles (17.8km)	295ft (90m)	5 hrs

Comments

The National Trust's Horsey estate boasts an impressive windpump, an important fenland nature reserve as well as a fine stretch of beach, all visited here.

Field tracks and secluded lanes feature in this easy walk, starting from a 12th-century Benedictine priory.

The moated Oxburgh Hall is one of the most picturesque stately houses in Norfolk and offers a relaxing visit at the end of this gentle country walk.

Medieval Loddon grew rich from the surrounding farms and its splendid church and massive tithe barn at nearby Hales, linked by this ramble, demonstrate the bounteous productivity of the land.

Field tracks and a riverside path contrast with a dense fenland nature reserve, where birds, butterflies and perhaps even a deer are all to be seen at the right time of year.

Woodland nature reserves and old grazing commons bring a diversity of plant and animal life. They are brought together on this walk, which also includes two of Norfolk's noted churches.

The National Trust's Felbrigg is noted, not only for its fine house, but an extensive woodland estate, part of which is incorporated in this excursion to nearby Metton.

Norfolk's Breckland is special; a sandy, sparsely wooded heath favouring an astonishing variety of flowers. The walk also wanders within the fringes of Thetford Forest to discover the Devil's Punchbowl.

The Broads marshes encompass many different types of habitat and this walk takes in something of them all, with glimpses of open water, reed beds, winding river, grazing meadows and wet woodland.

The story of the fenmen is told in a restored cottage at How Hill, the walk introducing some of the landscapes that were important to a lost way of life.

A relaxing countryside ramble links these two pretty Norfolk villages, one set around a contender for the largest green in the country, the other preserving its original early medieval plan.

The Broads are traditionally visited by boat, but after strolling past a remote country church, this walk takes a landman's view from a waterside path along one of the less frequented rivers.

Acres of mixed woodland contrast with fabulous water meadows beside the River Bure on this wander around the Blickling estate, where a visit to the hall and gardens will complete the perfect day.

The Peddars Way is based on a Roman road and ancient trackway and strikes an almost dead-straight line right across the county. Try this short section for a taster, centred on the tiny village of Fring.

Adjacent monastic houses and one of the country's most spectacular earthwork defences are linked on this picturesque circuit that wanders along the shallow upper valley of the River Nar.

A delightful route that straddles Boudica's Way, a long distance path remembering the queen of the Iceni who defied the might of the Roman occupation.

Unusual pools created in the last Ice Age, a Roman road and a very pleasant disused railway line are featured on this relaxing wander through some of Norfolk's prettiest countryside.

Scattered copses and woods are one of the distinctive features of the Norfolk landscape and if you can time this ramble for a warm autumn day, you are in for a real treat.

Norfolk's north-east corner is bounded by a run of high cliffs overlooking superb beaches and backed by inland hills that rise to the county's highest point.

The pattern of Norfolk's northern coastline results from man's efforts to claim coastal farmland during the 18th century, as this walk along the sea defences around Blakeney vividly demonstrates.

Windmills and watermills conjure some of the most romantic images of the English countryside and this walk is well blessed, for it includes two of each as well as a splendid stretch of Norfolk coast.

This walk between three main rivers leads to the Denver Sluice, a navigable gateway between the higher reaches and the sea and a vital control in maintaining the delicate balance of water levels.

Explore the salt marshes from a popular seaside resort, before turning to quiet villages in the gentle hills behind, passing an imposing Iron Age ring fort; its ancient defences a formidable sight.

The Berney Arms must be one of the country's least accessible pubs, making the challenge of getting there all the more worthwhile. This route crosses a vast expanse of open marsh past several windpumps.

Disused railways have fostered many recreational paths, but this stretch of the Marriott's Way must be one of the prettiest. Old by-ways extend the walk to the magnificent medieval church at Salle.

Hidden within the great Thetford Forest, Grime's Graves is one of the most important prehistoric sites in Britain and this walk to it follows a very beautiful stretch of the Little Ouse River.

From a pretty village, dominated by an impressive Norman castle, this walk rambles through woodland onto a rare heathland landscape, which supports a rich diversity of plant and wildlife.

A succession of nature reserves reveal salt marsh, dune and grassland down, where bird spotters, plant lovers or those simply out to enjoy the views will all find plenty of interest.

Keymap

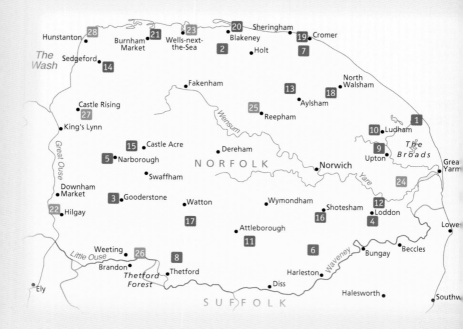

Pleasant track across the countryside

Introduction to Norfolk

If you've never been to Norfolk, you are in for a real surprise, for the popular image that it is monotonously flat and uninteresting is a complete myth. The author of one 1930s guide to Britain more accurately hit the mark, when he wrote of the peaceful beauty of the inland landscape and the best preserved county in England. Seventy years on, his comments still hold true for, set in and around its gently undulating hills, you will find one of the most unspoiled countrysides in England.

A lack of mineral wealth in coal and iron tended to isolate Norfolk as Britain's 19th-century Industrial Revolution gathered pace and, not being on the road to anywhere, left it a place to be visited only by those with some purpose. As a consequence, its peacefully detached, rural way of life continued far longer than in many other counties. Even now, no motorways connect it to the main industrial and commercial centres and, for the most part, its towns and villages have escaped the charmless sprawl of development that afflicts so much of England. That is not to say that Norfolk has not embraced 21st-century life, but you do not have to wander far to find tranquil open space, picturesque villages and quiet by-ways.

Wildlife Habitats

There is a surprising diversity of terrain within its borders. True, there are areas that are flat and indeed below sea level, but there is nothing monotonous about the landscape even here. The Broads, the stranger's concept of all that Norfolk has to offer, resulted from the flooding of vast peat diggings, worked from prehistoric times right through the Middle Ages. Today the maze of sluggish waterways is not only a boaters' paradise, but also one of the richest wildlife areas of the country. Countless species of birds, plants and insects, many of them quite rare, such as the marsh harrier and swallowtail butterfly, are to be found in the woods, reed beds and water meadows that fringe the rivers and pools. The Broads' exceptional qualities have now been recognised in its designation as a National Park.

Much of the coastline is equally rewarding and falls within an Area of Outstanding Natural Beauty, a slightly anomalous title in that it too has been largely influenced by Man and is preserved in a delicate balance by his efforts. Although much of the coastal plain has been drained for farming, its salt marshes, dunes and siltings attract massive flocks of migrating, wintering and resident birds. Emphasising their importance, the country's first Wildlife Trust Reserve was founded near Cley in 1926 which, incidentally, is one of the first places where the elusive bittern returned to breed. More nature reserves were subsequently established along the coast amongst the reclaimed marshes and fens, which have their own individual character. They possess a special, almost intangible quality, where vast skies, the strange perspective of a near horizon and the breeze rustling the reeds all combine to create a haunting and mysterious atmosphere.

Wander inland and you will find a similar wealth of wildlife habitats in the woods and forests, downs and meadows, heath and carr of Norfolk. For example, one of the village commons has a large colony of the pretty green-winged orchid. Stand on any low hill and all around, numerous copses and spinneys break the geometry of the endless fields. Few, if any, are remnants of the primeval forest that once spread across the country, but have been managed over the centuries to provide timber for fuel, construction and a host of manufacturing purposes from matchstick-making to boat building. Others were planted as windbreaks providing some protection to the fields from the 'Norfolk Blows', the unremitting winds that can raise spring dust storms from the friable tilled earth.

Denver Mill

All, however, contain a rich bio-diversity and give cover for many animals and birds. Norfolk retains significant areas of open heath, and the Brecklands, a fascinating region to explore, is one of the largest remaining expanses in the country. Their impoverished soils, abandoned to grazing for centuries, have become refuges for a wide range of delicate flora, whilst in the damper areas, carrs or wetland woods have their own unique array of plants and animals.

Early History

History has left its mark upon the land, right from the dawn of time. The earliest prehistoric immigrants after the last Ice Age made their way through the surrounding marshes to colonise the islands and high ground. In the heart of the Brecks, at Grime's Graves, they mined the underlying flint on such a scale that it is recognised as the first industrial site in the country. Later, the light, sandy soils and chalk downs, once they had been cleared of woodland, lent themselves to early agriculture. This corner of the country became the stronghold of the Iceni who, under the leadership of their queen, Boudica, dared defy the military might of the Roman occupation. Whilst the rebellion was short-lived, her legend lives on as do the outlines of several of their forts and settlements, the most impressive standing on a hill above Warham on the north coast. The Romans subsequently adopted a more conciliatory approach in their rule and left their mark in military roads, like the Peddars Way, which still marches across the landscape, and coastal forts, built to defend the shores against attacks by raiding Saxon brigands. They also took the first tentative steps in controlling the waterscape by digging ditches and straightening rivers to render them more navigable.

Walking through the dunes

Drainage

Little more was done until the 17th century, when the expertise of Dutch engineers was employed to drain the fens above King's Lynn. A 21-mile channel from Earith to Denver revealed the potential for land reclamation there and around the coast, setting a pattern of ditch digging and embankment raising that has continued unabated to this day. It immediately became apparent that drainage was, by itself, not enough, and windpumps sprang up across the countryside to lift water from the fields, steadily sinking as the ground dried out, to the rivers above. The process has continued, with each generation renewing or heightening the banks and calling upon ever more powerful and reliable pumps to push the water out to the sea. Many of the old drainage towers nostalgically dot the fenland, but the endless work of removing water and controlling levels is now undertaken by automated electric pumps and sluices.

Medieval Economy

Farming has always been a mainstay of Norfolk's economy and during the medieval period it became one of the richest counties in England. Wool and grain were important commodities and here the land was truly bountiful. The produce was shipped to London and elsewhere, but even more importantly, a lucrative trade developed across the

North Sea with the Low Countries. Bustling ports sprang up around the coast and Flemish weavers came to establish a flourishing textile industry. The influx of ideas influenced buildings too, introducing the use of brickwork and roofing tiles and the incorporation of decorative touches such as Dutch gabling.

The area is almost devoid of suitable building stone and any utilised had to be imported, generally from the Barnack quarries in Northamptonshire, making it prohibitively expensive. Vernacular architecture, therefore, developed around the use of the plentiful flint and cobbles for walls and thatch for roofing, a style that has created the many attractive villages. Such materials are, however, unsuitable for making corners and the early churches were frequently built with round towers, an endearing feature more or less confined to East Anglia. But the churches of the Middle Ages often have a very different character, for by then, Norfolk had grown rich on the profits of wool. Eager benefactors wishing to make provision for their place in the world to come, funded the construction of massive and ornately decorated churches. Norwich alone has fifty as well as a spectacular cathedral and a large number of the tiny villages cluster around a magnificent and richly furnished building.

Exploration

Like many areas, Norfolk is best explored on foot, enabling a full appreciation of the countryside and its features. Everywhere the walking is easy with no significant hills or forbidding terrain and you will find that the footpaths and stiles are generally well maintained and signed. The snaking, raised embankments of the fens and the gentle swells of the hills open up ever-changing vistas and you rarely have to walk far to enjoy a completely different scene. Wherever they go, bird watchers and flower lovers will be in their element, the changing seasons constantly bringing something new. There is no shortage of pretty villages, castles, fine country houses and churches to discover, whilst those simply seeking peace and solitude can lose themselves in a timeless landscape. This collection of walks explores some of the finest corners of this beautiful county, but can by no means be inclusive and will hopefully encourage you to wander further.

This book includes a list of waypoints alongside the description of the walk, so that you can enjoy the full benefits of gps should you wish to. For more information on using your gps, read the Pathfinder® Guide *GPS for Walkers*, by gps teacher and navigation trainer, Clive Thomas (ISBN 978-0-7117-4445-5). For essential information on map reading and basic navigation, read the Pathfinder® Guide *Map Reading Skills* by outdoor writer, Terry Marsh (ISBN 978-0-7117-4978-8). Both titles are available in bookshops or can be ordered online at www.crimsonpublishing.co.uk

At the edge of the Upton
Fen Nature Reserve

Horsey

Start

Horsey Windpump

Distance

3¾ miles (6km)

Height gain

Negligible

Approximate time

1½ hours

Route terrain

Field paths, dunes and a quiet lane

P Parking

National Trust car park (pay and display)

Dog friendly

Dogs on leads when seals on beach

OS maps

Landranger 134 (Norwich & The Broads), Explorer OL40 (The Broads)

GPS waypoints

TG 457 222
Ⓐ TG 462 222
Ⓑ TG 462 227
Ⓒ TG 472 233
Ⓓ TG 464 241
Ⓔ TG 459 236

Starting at one of the best-preserved drainage mills in Norfolk, this fascinating walk explores a coastal nature reserve where the lonely beach is home to a large colony of Atlantic grey seals.

Horsey Mere and Windpump

By the time the Horsey Windpump was built in 1912, steam engines were already taking over the job of draining the fens and one was installed here as a reserve should the water rise too quickly or the wind fail at a critical moment. Nevertheless, the windpump continued to operate until struck by lightening in 1943.

Horsey Mere, together with its surrounding marshes and woodland, is an important bird reserve and attracts large numbers of birds throughout the year. Amongst the rarer species that breed here are Cetti's warbler and the bittern. The best view of Horsey Mere is to be had from the end of a path that leaves the windpump along the southern bank of the staithe, but you must return to the car park to begin the walk.

Cross the road from the car park entrance to a bridged ditch and clamber over the stile in front to walk away at the edge of rough grazing. To the south, the distant view is to the Blood Hill Wind Farm at West Somerton, its regimented ranks of high-tech windmills a sharp contrast to the nostalgia of an earlier age. Reaching the corner Ⓐ, go over another stile beside a gate on the left. Follow a grass track that angles between the fields and eventually leads to a narrow lane Ⓑ.

The **Nelson Head** lies a short distance to the left although the onward route is to the right. Approaching the houses at Crinkle Hill, fork left past a barrier along a gravel track that heads towards the coast. Continue through a gate to Crinkle Gap Ⓒ, a break in the massive concrete and sand dune barrier that

Atlantic grey seals

This stretch of coast is home to one of the largest breeding colonies of Atlantic grey seals in the country and they frequently leave the water at low tide to bask on the beach. Recent years have seen a steady increase in the population and in 2009/10 some 300 pups were born. Pupping takes place during December and January and, being unable to swim for three or four weeks, the suckling seals lie above the tide line awaiting the return of their mothers. It is important that they are not disturbed during this period, but there is a safe viewing platform reached by following the track behind the dunes to the right of Ⓒ for ¼ mile.

protects the land from inundation.

The onward route lies to the left, either following the track behind the dunes if the tide is in (and during the pupping season) or through the gap and along the beach over a succession of groynes for ¾ mile. Reaching a second break in the dunes, the Horsey Gap **D**, turn inland to a car park. Walk out along its access drive to the corner of a lane.

Turn right, but leave after 100 yds along an unmarked path to the left **E** between the fields. At the far end, the way develops as a track, leading past houses to All Saints' Church.

A delightful thatched building of flint rubble, it dates back to the Saxon era. The original round tower, one of more than 120 in Norfolk, was transformed into an octagonal belfry at the

Seals basking on the coast

beginning of the 16th century.

Swing left at the corner by the church and then take the first right out to the main lane. Cross and go right along the verge, the path shortly slipping through the hedge into the adjacent field to take you beyond the village back to Horsey Windpump. ●

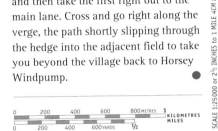

SCALE 1:25 000 or 2½ INCHES to 1 MILE *4CM to 1KM*

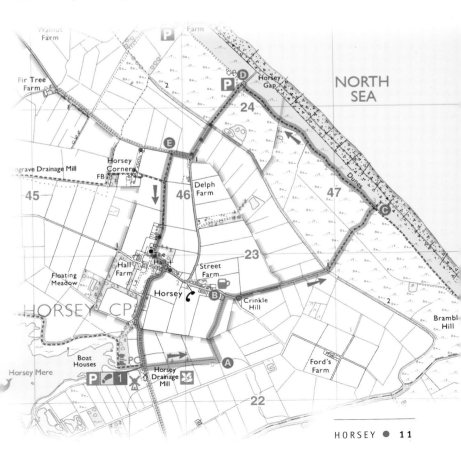

walk 2

Start
Binham

Distance
4¼ miles (6.9km)

Height gain
165 feet (50m)

Approximate time
2 hours

Route terrain
Field paths, tracks and quiet lanes

Parking
Car park at Binham Priory

OS maps
Landranger 132 (North West Norfolk), Explorer 251 (Norfolk Coast Central)

GPS waypoints
- TF 981 399
- Ⓐ TF 983 399
- Ⓑ TF 978 411
- Ⓒ TF 965 408
- Ⓓ TF 966 397
- Ⓔ TF 981 393

Binham Priory

An easy walk that is ideal for an afternoon stroll, the route following field tracks and secluded lanes around the small village of Binham. This attractive settlement is the site of a medieval Benedictine priory, whose impressive remains which include the parish church, can be freely visited.

Enter the graveyard in front of the church and walk through the ruined cloisters to leave the precincts of the remains through a gate in the perimeter fence near the chapter house. Bearing left, head due east across the field, making for a stile at the far side, just right of a group of trees. Reaching the lane beyond turn left, the way signed towards Stiffkey Ⓐ.

Cross a stream, which later flows into the River Stiffkey, and head up out of the village. At the top of the rise, the lane swings left and then, a little farther on, right. Leave at that point along a broad gravel track, Haystack Lane Ⓑ. It undulates onwards between expansive fields, enabling a pleasant panorama south across the valley. The way leads down to pass behind a farm. Where the track then swings right, keep ahead to a stile next to a gate. Continue at the field edge and then along a grass track, which runs beside the river to a bridge Ⓒ.

Ruins of Binham Priory

Binham

The village began as a Saxon settlement in the 6th century, but after the Norman invasion, William gave the manor to a nephew, Peter de Valoines, who founded the Benedictine priory in 1091. It was some time before work began on the priory church and its associated buildings, which took about 150 years to complete. From its size alone, it was obviously a wealthy community but, by all accounts, many of the priors were unscrupulous, one of them having to flee because of unpaid debts. These dubious activities were used by Henry VIII to legitimise the eviction of the monks in 1539. The monastic buildings were dismantled, the lead and timbers being sold off, but the western end of the great church was left. The reason being that, although the eastern portion of the church was for the private devotions of the monks, the nave west of the transept had always served the common folk of the parish. The village outside the precincts no doubt benefited from trade attracted by the priory and was granted a charter to hold an annual fair in 1107. An impressive 15th-century cross still stands at the eastern end of the village, although the green on which it stands was much larger then.

Cross and strike directly away over a couple of fields to emerge at a junction of lanes. Go along the one opposite and climb past Short Lane Farm, continuing on a gravel track to reach another lane. Turn left and walk past Ellis Farm to a bend, there branching off at a footpath sign into a field on the right **D**.

A cleared path through the crop conducts you across the field to the corner of a hedge at the top. Carry on beside it along a grass track, which, becoming hedged, runs between the fields, first as Lousybush Lane and then later, as Hall Lane. In due course the track ends at the bend of a lane outside the village. Follow it ahead, but after some 50 yds, abandon it in favour of a grass track on the left **E**. It passes behind the houses, emerging at the top through a converted farm. Joining the lane, walk left past the village hall back to the priory. ●

Oxborough and Gooderstone

Start
Oxborough

Distance
5 miles (8km)

Height gain
Negligible

Approximate time
2 hours

Route terrain
Field paths, tracks and quiet lanes

Parking
Roadside parking in village

OS maps
Landranger 143 (Ely & Wisbech), Explorer 236 (King's Lynn, Downham Market & Swaffham)

GPS waypoints
TF 744 014
Ⓐ TF 735 025
Ⓑ TF 743 033
Ⓒ TF 758 038
Ⓓ TF 762 025
Ⓔ TF 753 019

Oxburgh Hall is one of the prettiest country houses cared for by the National Trust and, with its tearoom, makes a superb focus for this pleasant stroll. It follows farm tracks, field paths and an occasional quiet lane, where riverside woods contrast with open views across the fields.

Oxborough

By the time work began on Oxburgh Hall in 1482, the need for massive defensive houses was becoming a thing of the past. However, imposing mansions reflected the status of the owner and with its wide moat and formidable embattled gatehouse, Sir Edmund Bedingfeld created a true impression of power. He served his king well in the Wars of the Roses to be rewarded with honours and, in return, entertained Henry VII at the hall in 1487. Oxborough church has two remarkable terracotta screens. Such Renaissance craftsmanship is rare in England and it is thought to have been executed around 1525 by craftsmen trained in Italy. That the chapel survives is a miracle, because in 1948, the spire, erected only 70 years earlier, suddenly collapsed bringing down with it the greater part of the church.

The walk begins from a junction by the corner of St John's Church, crossing the main road to a minor lane, Eastmoor Road. Follow it north out of the village, later curving past a row of cottages and continuing a further ¼ mile to Eastmoor Bridge Ⓐ. Leave the lane immediately before it at a footpath sign, passing through a gate on the right. Head upstream at the edge of an open wooded meadow. Eventually exiting at the far corner over a stiled footbridge, bear right past a field pond and across a couple of small pastures to a gate and stile at the corner of a small wood. The right of way maintains the same direction across the ensuing crop field to its far corner, but if this appears daunting, a track to the right follows its perimeter to the same place Ⓑ.

The ongoing track leads past Caldecote Farm onto a lane, where you should continue ahead for just over ¼ mile to a sharp right-hand bend. Leave there along the broad ongoing track, ignoring the first track, soon passed off to the right. Farther on, however, at a second junction Ⓒ, the main track swings right and follows a brake of Scots pine to a cottage, Folly Barn. Carry on forward, eventually reaching a lane, there turning right and then off left into Clarks Lane Ⓓ. That in turn leads into Gooderstone, ending in the village almost opposite **The Swan**. Observant walkers will have already noticed that Oxborough village carries a different spelling from that of the hall, a confusion that is perpetuated here, where this end of the lane is signed 'Clarke's Lane'.

> **Gooderstone** As in all the best villages, the two most important institutions in celebrating life's great milestones, church and pub, stand together in mutual convenience. Not to be outdone by neighbouring Oxborough, this 13th-century church too contains much of interest. There is a remarkable wooden screen across the chancel incorporating 16 painted panels and some fine carving decorating the pews. Unfortunately all the sculptured figures have been decapitated at the waist, but we can still appreciate the maker's inventiveness in the back panels, each of which is fretted in a different pattern.

The way through the village lies to the west (turn right as you emerge from Clarke's Lane), continuing later around a bend past Chalkrow Lane. However, just beyond, over the bridge and immediately past the entrance to a small water treatment plant, mount a stile on the left into the corner of a field **E**. Strike out across rough pasture to another stile at the far-right corner then keep ahead with an accompanying hedge on your left. At its eventual end by Church Farm, walk forward with a beech hedge now on your right. Approaching the corner, climb a stile on the right, from which a contained path leads out to a track from the farm. Go left back to the church.

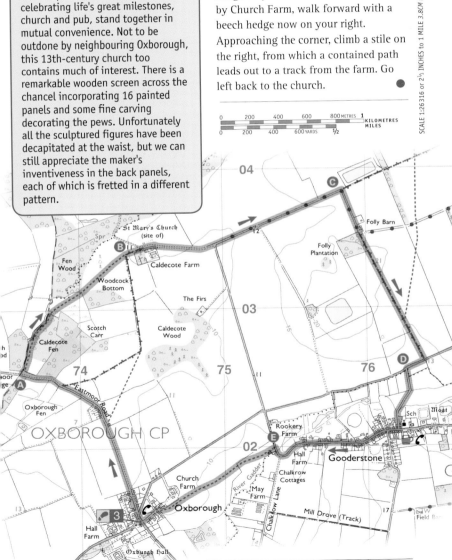

SCALE 1:26316 or 2⅖ INCHES to 1 MILE 3.8CM to 1KM

Start
Loddon

Distance
5¼ miles (8.4km)

Height gain
165 feet (50m)

Approximate time
2½ hours

Route terrain
Field paths, tracks and quiet lanes

P Parking
Car park near church (pay and display)

OS maps
Landranger 134 (Norwich & The Broads), Explorer OL40 (The Broads)

GPS waypoints

TM 362 987
Ⓐ TM 364 983
Ⓑ TM 366 973
Ⓒ TM 370 959
Ⓓ TM 367 961
Ⓔ TM 357 972

Hales Green from Loddon

Old field paths and tracks define the route of this pleasant, countryside ramble, which links Loddon to some of the rich manor farms that contributed to its medieval prosperity. Hales Hall is a fine example and, when open, the gardens and tithe barn provide an interesting break during the walk.

Loddon proudly traces its history to around AD 630 and grew as a focus of agriculture and trade. Its church, a reflection of the town's medieval wealth, was built towards the end of the 15th century by Sir James Hobart of nearby Hales, who rose to prominence as Attorney General to Henry VII.

Walk from the car park into the churchyard and swing right in front of the south porch. Leave along a contained path that runs behind the gardens of the buildings lining Loddon's main street. At the end, go left, the road shortly taking you over a brook. Turn off immediately after the bridge Ⓐ on a signposted footpath that follows the bank upstream. Reaching the main road, cross to a field path opposite, which continues along the shallow grass valley below an extensive bank pockmarked with rabbit holes, Warren Hills. Eventually reaching a fence, leave through a pinch stile over to the left Ⓑ.

The way immediately forks, with the left branch rising directly out of the valley as an old, hedged path that ends at the corner of a track by Loddon Hall. Walk forward, but turn left just before the entrance along a green swathe. At the corner, swing right and then, over a stile go right again, skirting the boundary hedge and passing the village cricket green. Cross the main drive to the house and carry on, soon joining a gravel track running along Hales Green. Keep ahead past Transport Lane and again where the track finally turns into Cowslip

Hales Hall and barn Built in 1480 by Sir James Hobart, the brick-built barn is Norfolk's largest, with walls some 2½ feet thick. It was built as a massive storehouse and a place of work, enabling the sheaves of wheat to be threshed by hand flails under cover during the autumn and winter following the harvest. The gardens are set within the original Tudor walls and are bounded by a carp-filled moat.
To visit the barn and the gardens, when open, take the left fork after the cattle-grid to the garden centre where you can buy entrance tickets.

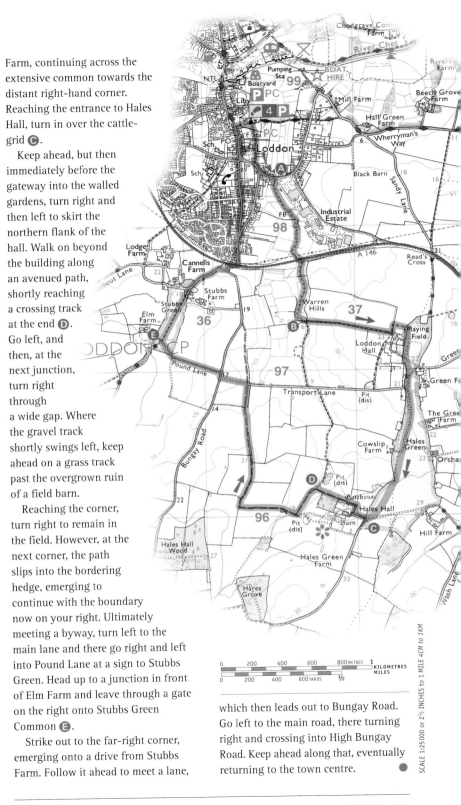

Farm, continuing across the extensive common towards the distant right-hand corner. Reaching the entrance to Hales Hall, turn in over the cattle-grid **C**.

Keep ahead, but then immediately before the gateway into the walled gardens, turn right and then left to skirt the northern flank of the hall. Walk on beyond the building along an avenued path, shortly reaching a crossing track at the end **D**. Go left, and then, at the next junction, turn right through a wide gap. Where the gravel track shortly swings left, keep ahead on a grass track past the overgrown ruin of a field barn.

Reaching the corner, turn right to remain in the field. However, at the next corner, the path slips into the bordering hedge, emerging to continue with the boundary now on your right. Ultimately meeting a byway, turn left to the main lane and there go right and left into Pound Lane at a sign to Stubbs Green. Head up to a junction in front of Elm Farm and leave through a gate on the right onto Stubbs Green Common **E**.

Strike out to the far-right corner, emerging onto a drive from Stubbs Farm. Follow it ahead to meet a lane, which then leads out to Bungay Road. Go left to the main road, there turning right and crossing into High Bungay Road. Keep ahead along that, eventually returning to the town centre. ●

walk 5

Start
Narborough

Distance
5½ miles (8.9km)

Height gain
Negligible

Approximate time
2½ hours

Route terrain
Woodland, field and riverside paths; short road section

P Parking
Lay-by behind bus shelter at the centre of Narborough

OS maps
Landranger 143 (Ely & Wisbech), Explorer 236 (King's Lynn, Downham Market & Swaffham)

GPS waypoints
- TF 750 127
- Ⓐ TF 740 125
- Ⓑ TF 730 114
- Ⓒ TF 718 108
- Ⓓ TF 723 119

Marham Fen and the Nar Valley Way

The River Nar is here flanked by productive farmland won from the drained marsh. The walk leaves the town, to which the river gives its name, crossing fields to an island of wetland wood nature reserve before returning along a peaceful riverbank.

Much of present-day Narborough stands back from the river, although the waterway was the source of its wealth during the 18th and 19th centuries. By 1759, the Nar had been made navigable as high as West Acre, enabling trade in grain, coal and gravel dug from the river valley. A large grist mill was built around 1780, with a 14-feet wheel that drove six separate millstones. The mill was extended in 1845 and continued to operate into the early 1950s. The newer section was poorly built and part of the roof collapsed in 1980, but restoration work has been undertaken and much of the original machinery survives. You will see the mill from across the river towards the end of the walk.

Cross the main road from the bus shelter to follow Meadow Close opposite, the street marked to Dennys Walk and Old Vicarage Park. Passing a junction at the edge of the village, continue forward along a narrow country lane, Meadow Road. The metalled way then shortly bends to the left, but again keep ahead, now on a gravel track. After crossing a stream, it curves around the perimeter of a small wood. Leave there by a gate on the left Ⓐ along a contained path across open fields towards a belt of pine. Pass through the trees and maintain your direction at the edge of successive fields, eventually crossing a bridge spanning a ditch. Beyond a final field the way emerges onto a concrete track Ⓑ.

Turn left and then, after 125 yds, go right, walking at the edge of a tangled old wood. Soon reaching a junction of tracks, continue along the one diagonally opposite through a gate. The track skirts the perimeter of Marham Fen, ultimately meeting another junction of tracks just inside a gate at the western entrance to the nature reserve Ⓒ.

Turn sharp right onto a path that cuts back through the heart of the fen, a thick impenetrable wet woodland once managed by coppicing, a practice no longer economically viable. The area is now a designated nature reserve, its pools and wooded bogs rich in varied plant life, which, in turn encourages butterflies such as brimstone and orange tip.

Emerging at the far side of the fen take the track ahead, which follows the edge of a large open field to a riverside pumping station **D**. Walk forward and then swing right to gain the raised bank, built to contain the course of the Nar, and follow it to the right. Wildlife is plentiful here too; in early spring hares frolic in the fields, whilst along the river there are swans, herons, and even the occasional kingfisher.

Approaching the village, the river passes between brick pillars that once carried the railway across the valley. Beyond, the watercourse divides, that to the left being the tailrace from the large grist mill, which now comes into view. The path, however, runs beside the overflow channel before turning away between gardens to emerge onto the end of a street. Follow it out to the main road and turn right back to the start. ●

Nar Bone Mill

On the opposite bank of the River Nar ½ mile beyond **D**, is the ruin of a bone mill, built in the 19th century. Crushed bone was in demand as an agricultural fertiliser and bones were hauled upriver on barges from King's Lynn. The bones were largely a by-product from the whaling industry there, but after this finished in 1821, the raw material came from slaughterhouses and even exhumations from German cemeteries. Before crushing, the bones would be boiled, an unsociable process that partly explains its remote location. The bags of fertiliser were then shipped back to King's Lynn, or taken upriver to the railway once this began operating. However, during the 1880s the river navigation became absorbed within a drainage scheme and the Nar was eventually shut off from the main river by a sluice at King's Lynn. Isolated from the sea, trade declined and the mill closed shortly afterwards.

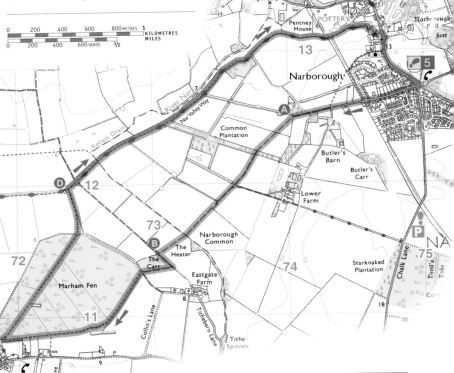

walk | 6

Tyrrel's Wood and Shelton

Start

Tyrrel's Wood on minor lane, 2 miles south of Long Stratton

Distance

5½ miles (8.9km)

Height gain

Negligible

Approximate time

2½ hours

Route terrain

Woodland and field paths, quiet lanes

Parking

Roadside car park

OS maps

Landrangers 134 (Norwich & The Broads) and 156 (Saxmundham), Explorers 230 (Diss & Harleston) and 237 (Norwich)

GPS waypoints

TM 205 893
Ⓐ TM 205 912
Ⓑ TM 211 916
Ⓒ TM 221 910
Ⓓ TM 227 906
Ⓔ TM 220 894

Small patches of woodland dot the Norfolk landscape and many, like Tyrrel's Wood where this walk begins, are accessible to the public. The walk then crosses an ancient common and returns over fields and along quiet lanes, visiting a couple of pleasant villages that boast remarkable churches.

A profusion of paths radiate through Tyrrel's Wood and you could easily spend a couple of hours pottering about in the trees. Its age has fostered a good mix of species, with many partial clearings where flowers take advantage of the sunlight filtering through the branches. Fallen boughs decay under fungal growths or are devoured by beetles and grubs, themselves food for small birds, which, as in most woodlands, are more often heard than seen.

A confident path heads into the trees, shortly splitting at a wayposted fork, where an Iceni spearhead defining Boudica's Way guides you left. Walk on to a bridge spanning a ditch, immediately after which go left. Reaching a fork bear right, soon passing a bench. There, leave the main path over another bridge on the left and swing right beside the ditch. At a

Along Wood Lane

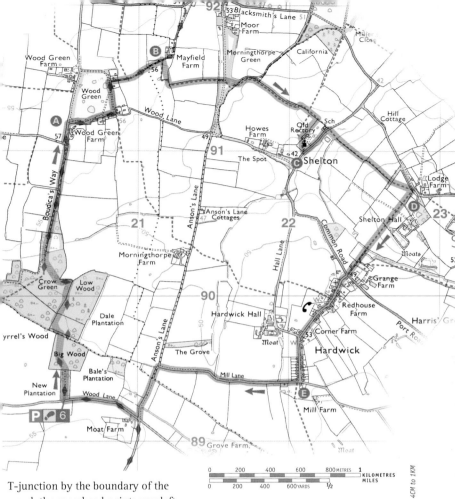

SCALE 1:25'000 or 2½ INCHES to 1 MILE 4CM to 1KM

T-junction by the boundary of the wood, the spearhead points you left, and then, at the next junction, right. Keep ahead as paths combine, before long leaving the wood on a track that leads out to a lane. Go right to pass Wood Green Farm. Immediately beyond the buildings, look for a waypost directing Boudica's Way off to the right **A**.

Walk away at the edge of a grass common, slipping through trees to join a track past cottages. On reaching a junction in front of a white house, go left, the way becoming a grass track. After passing a thatched cottage, turn right opposite a reedy pond, continuing across the fields behind the gardens towards Mayfield Farm. As the track becomes gravelled, there is a waypost beside the start of a hedge pointing into the right-hand field **B**.

Strike away towards an indented corner and, through a gap there, go left. Maintain your direction beyond the end of the boundary to a lane. Cross it and the bordering grass strip to a plank bridge in the far hedge and go left in the adjacent field. Where the hedge finishes, twist left and right across a ditch and continue with it on your right. Later, with the road in sight, come to a plank spanning the ditch. Over it, swing left and then right within the perimeter of a crop field, before slipping through a gap into the graveyard of Shelton's

Shelton family funerary monument

church. Walk around the building out to the lane **C**.

St Mary's, Shelton

St Mary's, is a large and impressive building; it was rebuilt during the Tudor period by the then lord of the manor, Sir Ralph Shelton, to replace a much earlier church mentioned in the Domesday Book. Sir Ralph was a prominent figure at Henry VIII's court, being the husband of Anne Boleyn's aunt. She looked after both of Henry's young princesses and it is said that Elizabeth was hidden in the church tower to protect her from arrest after her mother's execution. The Sheltons appear in the glass of the east window and Sir Ralph's motif, an 'R' with his surname played in the picture of a shell and tun (an old word for 'barrel'), appears everywhere.

Walk left up the lane past the former vicarage to the village school, turning off immediately beyond over a stile in the right-hand hedge. Cross a narrow enclosure to a gated bridge and keep forward at the subsequent field edge. Pass through a belt of trees and strike out across a rough pasture, swinging around within it to reach a stile by the distant right corner **D**.

Head directly away, passing the site of the old Shelton Hall over to the left. Continue across the next field to a stile at its far side and follow a track to emerge at the edge of Hardwick. Cross to the lane opposite and walk past the church, bereft of its round tower that collapsed during a storm in 1770.

Walk on through the village to a T-junction at the end of the lane **E**. Go right along Mill Lane, the way signed towards Pulham St Mary and Bush Green. Where that finishes turn left and then, at a crossroads, right into Wood Lane, heading finally towards Long Stratton and the car park. ●

St Margaret's, Hardwick

This church too is accepted as a Saxon foundation, the rounded head above the north door being a typical characteristic. Inside, on the north wall is a 14th-century painting of St Christopher, which, at one time, included a fisherman, tucked in the bottom corner. The vestry at the back of the church is housed within a Jacobean 'tester' pew complete with roof. It would originally have stood in the chancel for the private use of the squire and his family. The 15th-century rood screen, although damaged, has survived the Reformation better than most and carries a panel on the top added by the churchwardens, John Ebbers and Joseph Cock in 1661.

Felbrigg Park and Metton

The splendid 17th-century mansion at Felbrigg overlooks an extensive park, which serves as an excellent beginning to this enjoyable ramble through the rolling north Norfolk countryside. Field paths, tracks and quiet lanes lead to the neighbouring hamlet of Metton, returning across farmland and woodland plantations before skirting a picturesque lake below the hall.

Start
Felbrigg Hall

Distance
5¾ miles (9.3km)

Height gain
180 feet (55m)

Approximate time
2½ hours

Route terrain
Parkland and field paths; short sections along quiet lanes

Parking
National Trust car park (pay and display)

OS maps
Landranger 133 (North East Norfolk), Explorer 252 (Norfolk Coast East)

GPS waypoints
- TG 194 393
- Ⓐ TG 199 390
- Ⓑ TG 199 373
- Ⓒ TG 197 362
- Ⓓ TG 193 371
- Ⓔ TG 188 382

Felbrigg Hall Although the present mansion dates only from the 1620s, the history of the Felbrigg estate begins in the 11th century when it was held by a powerful Norman baron, Roger Bigood. The first house was built by a descendant in the 13th century, who took the name of the manor as his own. The property was bought by John Wyndham, a successful if unscrupulous merchant from Wymondham, in 1461. Several descendants rose to prominent positions at court and were skilful in remaining a step ahead in political manoeuvrings. However, one Sir John did come unstuck and was separated from his head in 1502 for backing the Earl of Suffolk. The estate remained within the family until it was bequeathed to the National Trust in 1969 by Robert Wyndham Ketton-Cremer. When his father came to the house in 1923, the place was in need of massive repair. Undaunted, he set about the task of restoration. Robert continued the work until his death, being particularly interested in re-establishing the woods and plantations. The house, gardens and Great Wood are a tribute to his dedication.

Walk towards the information board at the end of the car park near the house and bear left through a gate along a track across the park towards the church of St Margaret. Rebuilt by the Felbriggs in the 15th century, it serves the parish but now stands well isolated from its congregation. The reason for the abandonment of the original village has been lost in time and perhaps resulted from depopulation by plague in the middle of the 16th century or alternatively clearance by the Wyndhams to improve land productivity. Inside, a splendid collection of brasses depict the lords of the manor and their ladies over almost five centuries.

Amble through the churchyard and leave by a gate in the north-east corner. Turn right along the edge of a meadow, climbing onto a farm track at the far side Ⓐ. Go right again and walk to a junction at its end. Pass through a gap into the

Felbrigg Hall

open field facing you and strike ahead towards woodland. A path leads between the trees to meet a broader track. Cross diagonally left and continue briefly beside the wood to a fingerpost, there swinging left on a cleared path across the field. Reaching the distant boundary, climb consecutive stiles below an oak tree and bear left across the ensuing meadow past the end of a fenced ditch to a stiled bridge in the perimeter. Keep going across a paddock and at the edge of a cemetery to emerge opposite Metton's church **B**. The tower of St Andrew's Church stands semi-detached from the building and is pierced by a passageway, possibly created to enable ceremonial processions to encircle the church. Inside, by the door you will find the constable's truncheon, a hefty aid to peace-keeping in the 1830s.

Cross and carry on along the track beside the church. When it ends, swing left and right to continue with a loose hedge on your left, turning within the perimeter to find a stepped gap some 100 yds along. Drop into the adjacent field and stride away with the boundary on your right. Leave through a break in the corner but then curve right to pass through a second gap and walk away along a rough meadow to the corner of the right-hand hedge **C**.

Turn right beside the hedge to find a stile tucked into the top corner. Cross and follow a contained path left that soon leads into a farmyard. Wind right and head out along its access track, which ultimately ends at a lane **D**. Go right for some 300 yds to leave at a signpost over a bridged ditch on the left. Walk away between the fields, but reaching the far end of a hedge, slip through to continue on its other side. The way then dog-legs left and right, the boundary running on to finally emerge onto a lane. To the right it leads to a junction opposite Keeper's Cottage at the edge of the Felbrigg estate **E**.

Turn left, following the lane up through a wood for ¼ mile, abandoning it just before it breaks from the trees in favour of a path, marked as the

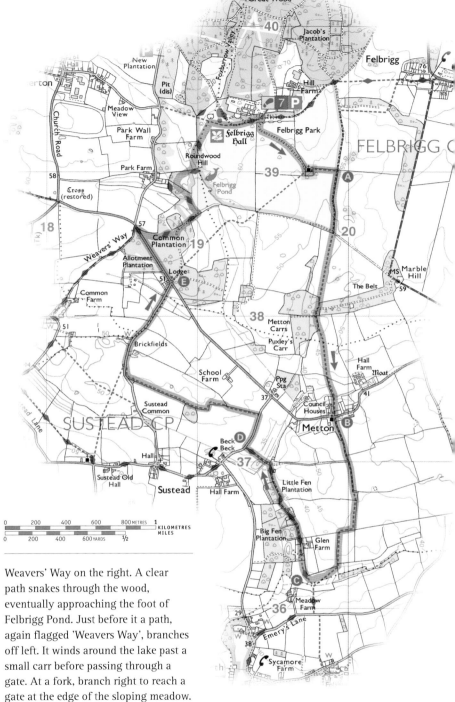

Weavers' Way on the right. A clear path snakes through the wood, eventually approaching the foot of Felbrigg Pond. Just before it a path, again flagged 'Weavers Way', branches off left. It winds around the lake past a small carr before passing through a gate. At a fork, branch right to reach a gate at the edge of the sloping meadow. A contained path dips across the stream feeding the lake and then swings left above the shallow valley. Reaching an ancient gnarled oak, leave through a

gate on the right. A grassy trod rises onto the park, joining a drive, which, to the right, takes you past the front of Felbrigg Hall back to the car park. ●

walk 8

Start

East Wretham Heath NWT Reserve, on A1075 3 miles north east of Thetford

Distance

6 miles (9.7km)

Height gain

Negligible

Approximate time

2½ hours

Route terrain

Forestry tracks and paths; short section along quiet lane

P Parking

NWT Reserve car park

Dog friendly

Dogs on leads through NWT Reserve

OS maps

Landranger 144 (Thetford & Diss), Explorer 229 (Thetford Forest in The Brecks)

GPS waypoints

TL 912 886
Ⓐ TL 903 883
Ⓑ TL 888 887
Ⓒ TL 877 893
Ⓓ TL 877 883
Ⓔ TL 890 882

Langmere and the Devil's Punchbowl

Beginning from a Breckland Norfolk Wildlife Trust Reserve, this walk wanders through a corner of Thetford Forest, passing some curious ponds or meres that fill and empty without regard to the seasons. There is always plenty of bird life about and, if you go quietly through the woods, you are likely to spot a deer or two.

The Brecks

Norfolk's Breckland is unique in the country. Farmed to exhaustion and then abandoned to heath, its poor, sandy soils provide little nutrition for plants and any that manage to grow must survive hot summers and cold winters with less rainfall than anywhere else in the country. Since the Middle Ages, much of the area has been grazed by sheep and the ubiquitous rabbit, originally introduced in conygers (warrens) to provide a ready source of meat and fur. Their constant nibbling keeps the grass in a sparse, short turf, from which tiny flowers, including forget-me-not and harebell, sprout. East Wretham was the Trust's first Breckland nature reserve. Established in 1938, it was almost immediately requisitioned and became part of a wartime airfield. Derelict ammunition stores are passed in the early stages of the walk and disintegrating runways have become a miniature rock garden for lichens, mosses and carpets of flowering plants such as wall bedstraw and yellow biting stonecrop.

A gate at the rear of the car park begins a path across the reserve, following occasional green and white topped-posts towards a pine wood. It was planted at the beginning of the 19th century and, unlike the commercial close-planted conifers, provides habitats for a number of different birds such as crossbills and redstarts. There are tawny owls here too and you may hear a great spotted

woodpecker drumming. Through a kissing-gate, keep ahead where the path forks, passing ruins of old bunkers shielded behind overgrown earth embankments, raised to minimise damage in case of an explosion. Over to the left, a hide looks across Langmere, which, when in water, attracts birds such as shoveler and little grebe, with waders probing at the muddy margins for food. The path winds on through the trees, eventually reaching a T-junction. Go left and leave the reserve through a gate onto a track, Harling Drove **A**.

Turn right through the main forest, a woodland mosaic reflecting different stages of commercial management. Mature trees are felled and new ones planted, although some corners may be left to natural regeneration, encouraging diversity in plant and wildlife. Much of this part of the forest is pine, but birch, gorse and occasional hawthorn grow here too. Keep ahead on the main track for a mile, eventually reaching a five-way junction **B**. Bear left slightly to keep with the main trail,

Grazing the heath

which immediately narrows through dense plantation. Continue for almost another ½ mile to a road junction. Carry on along the lane opposite, shortly arriving at a broad forest track and car park on the left **C**. Turn in past the Devil's Punchbowl.

Follow the onward track to a junction. Keep ahead, passing a cottage over on the left and then a barrier to continue on a forest trail. It ultimately

SCALE 1:25 000 or 2½ INCHES to 1 MILE 4CM to 1KM

0	200	400	600	800 METRES	1
					KILOMETRES
					MILES
0	200	400	600 YARDS	½	

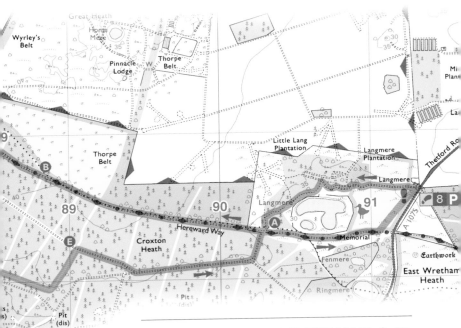

ends at a road **D**. Cross to another track opposite, which soon bends left

Devil's Punchbowl Like the East Wretham meres, the Devil's Punchbowl is fed by underground springs rather than rainfall and its level therefore depends on the subterranean water table. As winter rain soaks into the ground very gradually, it is often the case that the water is highest in midsummer. Such pools occur because the underlying rock is porous chalk, which is dissolved by the slight acidity of seeping rainwater to create underground fissures and caverns. These occasionally collapse creating depressions called dolines, of which the Devil's Punchbowl is the most dramatic example. At times it is completely dry but it has also been known to overflow onto the nearby road. The fluctuating water levels have created rings of different types of vegetation around the bowl and the water and mud are home to several rare species of beetle and freshwater shrimp.

around another deep but smaller pit. The way carries on beside beech at the edge of a replanted plot. Where the main forest road later swings right, remain ahead on a grass track. Keep going forward, over another crossway and past a couple of tracks off to the left. Later, bend left with the path and walk on until you reach a broad crossing track **E**.

Turn right, shortly passing through a large clearing where several tracks meet. Carry on ahead for another ½ mile to another main junction. There go left, emerging from the forest onto Harling Drove, just west of the point at which you originally joined it. Turn right, but instead of then going back through the gate, continue along the track past the southern edge of Langmere. Approaching the main road at the end, walk through a kissing-gate on the left and follow a waymarked trod at the edge of the heath back to the car park. ●

Devil's Punchbowl

River Bure and Upton Marshes

The Broadland marshes are a crucial haven for wildlife and encompass a wide range of different habitats: open water, grazing marsh, dense reed beds and wetland woods. Our route samples some of this great variety in South Walsham and Upton Marshes, starting along riverbanks and returning across fields to a deep woodland thicket.

walk 9

Start
South Walsham Broad
near Pilson Green

Distance
6 miles (9.7km)

Height gain
Negligible

Approximate time
2½ hours

Route terrain
Riverside and fenland
paths, a quiet lane

Parking
Car park near
moorings at South
Walsham Broad

OS maps
Landranger 134
(Norwich & The
Broads), Explorer
OL40 (The Broads)

GPS waypoints
🏁 TG 372 139
Ⓐ TG 379 156
Ⓑ TG 390 153
Ⓒ TG 389 148
Ⓓ TG 395 139
Ⓔ TG 397 134
Ⓕ TG 390 129
Ⓖ TG 379 136

Coming out of the car park, walk left along Fleet Lane past a series of private landings and a boatyard before the way narrows to a raised path beside Fleet Dike. Willows are important riverbank features, as are the 'ronds', fringes of reed beds lining the water. Tree roots help stabilise the artificial earthen embankments while the reed beds protect them from water erosion. To the left are the more extensive reed beds of Ranworth Flood, harvested in late winter for thatch. The 'floods' or lakes play an integral part in maintaining the delicate balance of water levels serving as reservoirs for rising waters backed up by incoming tides. Before long Fleet Dike is joined by another channel from the left and the path carries on past Ward Marsh to meet the River Bure Ⓐ.

The Bure is one of the major rivers draining the Broads and can be traced to a fold of gentle hills near Briston in north Norfolk. The raised path continues beside the main river,

St Benet's Abbey

Founded in 1020 under the Benedictine Order, St Benet's was the only monastery established within the county prior to the Norman Conquest. The monastic buildings stretched along the banks of the river towards the abbey church, the site of the high altar marked by a tall oaken cross that came from the Queen's Sandringham estate in 1987. The community managed to survive Henry VIII's purge and its last abbot, William Repps, became the Bishop of Norwich in 1536. The office of abbot continues to this day in the present bishop, who arrives by boat to preach a service in August each year. The abbey itself, however, was abandoned shortly after the Dissolution and the building fell into dereliction. Across the marshes, on a low hill to the east, stands St Edmund's thatched church at Thurne. In a room at the base of the tower, a small squint looks out over the fen to the abbey, where, it is said, a lantern was placed to send a signal to the monks in times of danger.

Sailing on Fleet Dike

overlooked on the opposite bank by the adjacent ruins of a drainage mill and the gatehouse of St Benet's Abbey.

Carry on beside the meandering river to the second drainage pump, Doles Pumping Station **B**. Drop from the riverbank to follow a broad track away. Where that subsequently swings left, turn off right in front of a field gate. Pass through an opening and wind left on a grass track bound by tall hawthorn. At its end **C**, go left along a narrower path, which later turns to the right. The path ultimately drops left to a gate and continues, flanked by ditches, to meet a concrete track at its end **D**.

A little over ¼ mile to the right, another track joins from the left. A few yards beyond that point, leave over a footbridge on the right **E**. Cross a second bridge and then bear left along a pleasant path bordering a tangled wood. Look out for swallowtail and white admiral butterflies and dragonflies such

as the Norfolk hawker. You might also see reed warblers or yellow wagtails in the fronded margins of the water. Meeting a lane at the edge of Upton, go right. After almost ½ mile and just before a cottage on the left, the Barn House, take a discretely signed track between house drives on the right **F**.

Narrowing to a grass trail, it leads to the edge of a wood and curves left beside it. Over a bridged ditch, the way shortly delves into the fringe of Upton Fen Nature Reserve. In early spring, the wood bursts into life with a bright show of flowers such as primrose and marsh marigold, followed later by the vivid yellow-topped spikes of flag iris. Reaching a gate into the carr, go left past fishing ponds to a farm. Swing right and walk out to a junction of lanes. Take the one going right, but leave opposite a cottage, just beyond a small car park, along a contained field-edge path **G**.

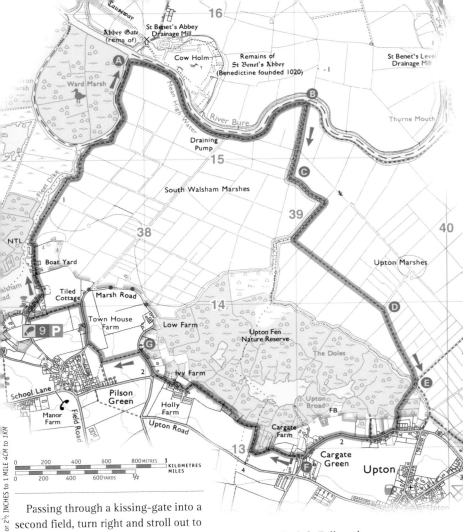

Passing through a kissing-gate into a second field, turn right and stroll out to a lane. Go right again, shortly reaching Town House Farm. Walk on for a further 100 yds before turning off through a gate gap on the left. Follow the boundary away, coming out on another lane almost opposite the car park. ●

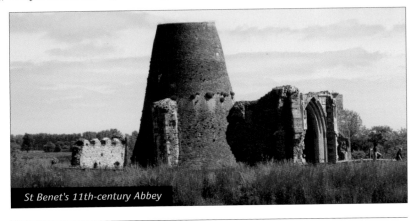

St Benet's 11th-century Abbey

SCALE 1:25000 or 2½ INCHES to 1 MILE 4CM to 1KM

Start
How Hill near Ludham

Distance
6 miles (9.7km)

Height gain
Negligible

Approximate time
2½ hours

Route terrain
Countryside paths and quiet lanes; brief section beside main road

Parking
Car park for Toad Hole Cottage

OS maps
Landranger 134 (Norwich & The Broads), Explorer OL40 (The Broads)

GPS waypoints
TG 372 189
Ⓐ TG 373 193
Ⓑ TG 380 188
Ⓒ TG 388 183
Ⓓ TG 388 178
Ⓔ TG 372 170

How Hill and Ludham

How Hill is the starting point for this delightful ramble, which culminates at a restored cottage housing an interesting museum of fen life. Rolling countryside fringing the marshes and an attractive town with an ancient church all combine to make a splendid afternoon's walk.

From the entrance of the car park turn left, following the lane over the crest of the hill past the How Hill Study Centre. The house is a genteel piece of Edwardian romanticism, built in 1905 by the successful Norwich architect, Edward Boardman.

Sailing on The Broads

He discovered the place on a boating holiday, bought the estate and built the magnificent thatched mansion overlooking the valley. Initially used only as a holiday retreat, Boardman and his family eventually settled here and sometime after his death it was developed as a study centre for young people.

Beyond, the leafy lane falls in a gentle slope, where you might see a red squirrel. At the bottom, leave opposite a house along a bridleway on the right Ⓐ. Walk away beside a hedge lined with oak, swinging left at the top and continuing to a junction. Turn right, ultimately coming out at the corner of a lane Ⓑ. Follow it left to a T-junction and go left again, the way signed to Catfield and Potter Heigham. Reaching an offset

crossroads, take the right branch, which leads out to the main road. Follow that left into Ludham, a hedged path on the right avoiding the road. Carry on to a crossing in the centre of the village by the thatched **tearoom**, adjacent pub (**King's Arms**) and church Ⓒ.

At the corner by the church, turn right. Follow the lane for a little over ¼ mile, crossing the staithe and shortly reaching Lovers Lane, on the right beside a cottage Ⓓ. Becoming a track, it leads into fields. At a later junction,

SCALE 1:25 000 or 2½ INCHES to 1 MILE 4CM to 1KM

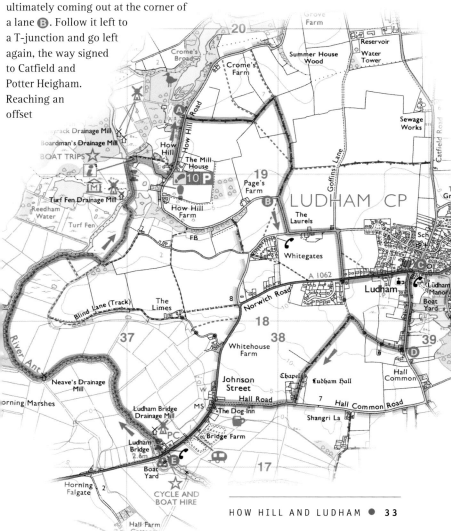

swing sharp left onto a bridleway, which rises to a farm at the top of the hill, Ludham Hall. Keep going through the yard and past the hall, dipping at the far side to meet a lane. The splendid Georgian front of the hall disguises a Jacobean origin, when the house and its associated chapel belonged to the bishops of Norwich.

Follow the lane right to the main road and there go left, using the pavement, down to Ludham Bridge **E**. Approaching the bridge, drop right beside the River Ant. Past moorings and the low, tilting stack of a drainage mill, bear from the river through a handgate along an embankment between open pools and reed beds, developed to encourage bitterns and other birds to breed. Disembodied sails float above a sea of swaying grass along the adjacent river, which describes a lazy loop towards How Hill. Eventually the path turns towards a copse of trees. At a junction there go left at the edge of the reed beds, passing gardens resplendent in early summer with the blooms of rhododendron and azalea.

Before long the path and riverbank reunite in front of Turf Fen Drainage Mill. Towards the far end of moorings, and before reaching a thatched boathouse, turn away over a footbridge to pass Toad Hole Cottage.

Beyond the cottage, bear right across a sloping lawn back to the car park. ●

How Hill

The earthwork defences of Castle Acre are formidable

walk 11

The Buckenhams

Start
Old Buckenham

Distance
6¼ miles (10km)

Height gain
100 feet (30m)

Approximate time
3 hours

Route terrain
Quiet lanes and field paths

Parking
Roadside parking in village

OS maps
Landranger 144 (Thetford & Diss), Explorer 237 (Norwich) & 230 (Diss & Harleston)

GPS waypoints
TM 064 915
Ⓐ TM 063 911
Ⓑ TM 056 904
Ⓒ TM 063 898
Ⓓ TM 085 903
Ⓔ TM 083 909
Ⓕ TM 076 915

Linking two settlements with the same name, this relaxing walk makes use of quiet lanes, field tracks and paths. Woodland and open common add to the beauty of the landscape, while a windmill, castle and attractive village buildings provide much of interest along the way.

Old Buckenham Mill

Old Buckenham has had as many as five mills in its time, for this was one of the main wheat producing areas in the county. However, the others were wooden post mills and have not survived and, indeed, this had become largely derelict before restoration began in the 1980s. Put up in 1818, it has the distinction of having the widest tower of any in the country, measuring 23 feet across the base and originally had eight sails to power five millstones. The mill was damaged during a storm in 1879 and, as part of the repairs, the sails were replaced with the more traditional four. It continued working until 1926, but closed when the miller, Billy Gooderman, could not afford necessary repairs. The size of the adjacent granary gives some idea of the volume of business and was constructed in 1856, with a bakehouse subsequently added.

Follow the main road from **The Gamekeeper** past the village pond and turn off right into The Green beside the expansive Church Green. *You can follow a trod across or walk around the perimeter, turning left at the next junction before a neat row of Victorian almshouses,* either way reaching the far corner of the green Ⓐ. Go right along Mill Road, passing cottages and the former granary, behind which stands Old Buckenham Mill. The entrance lies along the lane, just before the de-restriction sign, and it is open on the second Sunday of each month during spring and summer.

Carry on along Mill Road and over a crossroads towards Wilby and Eccles, shortly reaching another junction.

Go left and then shortly fork left along a gravel track marked as Sandy Lane **B**.

A broad avenue leads past a couple of houses and the entrance to Lodge Farm, continuing beyond within the fringe of a wood where colourful rhododendron flower in late spring. Meeting a lane at the far end, turn left and walk for almost ¼ mile to find a track, signed as a footpath, leaving on the right, just before the edge of the wood **C**.

Pass through the trees and keep going between fields, eventually arriving at a plank bridge on your left. Pass through the hedge and continue to the right beside it in the adjacent field to emerge onto another lane. Cross to a gate and stile opposite and carry on ahead, climbing a succession of stiles. In the final field, turn the corner and exit onto a lane. Go left, cross a junction and walk on towards the village of New Buckenham. The lane bends left and then right, at which point, a footpath leaves on the left, doubling back in front of a cottage, once St Mary's Chapel **D**.

The path leads to New Buckenham Castle, but to see it, you will first need the key. It can be obtained for a small charge from Castle Garage, just along the lane towards the village. After returning the key, continue into the centre of the village along King Street.

At the end of King Street turn left into Queen Street, walking beside the

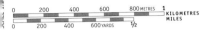

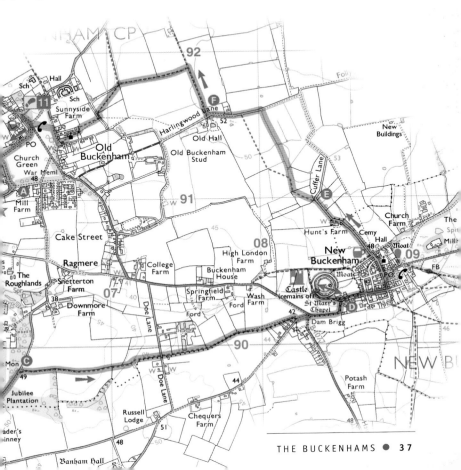

New Buckenham

Britain has many medieval towns, but New Buckenham is unique in that its original layout has not been overrun with later development. Despite their 18th or 19th-century appearance, many of the buildings lining the streets are in fact timber-frame houses, a number with overhanging upper floors. The 'market house', thought to have been a toll or court building, was set on Doric pillars around 1700, re-using timbers from earlier buildings. The curious central pillar is a whipping post; a reminder of the harsh summary justice once meted out to offenders. The castle dates from the mid 12th century and was constructed by William d'Albini when he moved his seat of power from Old Buckenham to take advantage of the trade between Thetford and Norwich. It is regarded as having the earliest and largest circular keep in the country, defended by a deep, water-filled moat and encircling earth embankment 40 ft high. Archaeological evidence suggests a more extensive complex once encompassed the town. St Martin's Church is also worth a look and contains a font decorated with carvings of lions and wild men, known as woodwoses.

market green into Church Street. Pass St Martin's and keep ahead by the cemetery along Cuffer Lane, going for just over ¼ mile to a sharp right-hand bend **E**. Leave the lane through a gate on the left, striking to another at the far corner of the field. Bearing right, a path cuts the crop and continues in the same direction at the edge of subsequent fields, eventually ending onto a lane. Go left and, after ¼ mile, turn off along a gravel track opposite Old Hall Farm, waymarked as the Tas Valley Way **F**.

After some ¼ mile, a signpost on the right indicates a path leaving on the left, which follows the uncultivated margin between open fields. Reaching the corner, drop over a plank bridge and go left to a stile. Strike a diagonal to the far corner of a paddock and walk a few paces left along a grass track to find another stile on the right. Cross a final paddock towards the church and then follow the edge of the cemetery into the churchyard, passing All Saints', which features an octagonal tower and thatched roof. Leave by a path to the right at the north-western corner onto a lane and turn right past **The Ox and Plough**. Bear left across the green to return to The Gamekeeper.

Old Buckenham Mill

Hardley Cross

walk 12

Start
Chedgrave

Distance
6½ miles (10.5km)

Height gain
80 feet (25m)

Approximate time
3 hours

Route terrain
Quiet lane and riverside path

Parking
All Saints' Church car park (but avoid service times)

OS maps
Landranger 134 (Norwich & The Broads), Explorer OL40 (The Broads)

GPS waypoints
TM 362 993
Ⓐ TG 388 011
Ⓑ TG 400 011
Ⓒ TM 387 996

The first section of the route offers easy walking along a quiet lane from Chedgrave to the River Yare, the low hill enabling a splendid view across the expansive flood plain to Yarmouth on the coast. The return follows the main river before turning up beside the River Chet, passing Hardley Flood, a tidal lake and nature reserve that attracts many waterbirds, particularly in winter.

Coming out of the church drive, follow Hardley Road to the right, quickly leaving the village behind. It undulates gently on for 1½ miles, offering a lovely view across the landscape. The distant factory is at Cantley, built to process sugar beet, one of the major crops grown in the area. The lane eventually leads to St Margaret's Church.

There must be a far-reaching view from the top of the round tower, but while sadly that is not accessible, you can at least look inside the church. The font displays some fine carving, while on the wall opposite the doorway is a painting depicting St Christopher. St Margaret's Church escaped the attentions of the Victorian restorers, and retains its old, plain benches, peppered with woodworm, and scratched with pictures of the ships that brought trade along the river.

Carry on beyond the church and bear left at a junction, dropping past a farm to Hardley Staithe Ⓐ. Take the path that runs along the right-hand side of the water, continuing beyond the moorings through a handgate along the raised embankment bordering Hardley Dike. It leads on for ¼ mile to the River Yare.

> **Hardley Dike** The channel was dug in the 19th century, replacing a much earlier, sinuous course and enabled boats to dock beside the small settlement. It would have been a busy spot and there was once a pub here to serve the boatmen. Cargoes would have included coal, bricks and other supplies for the village, the returning boats taking away the crops produced on the higher fields as well as reeds and willows cut from the marsh.

Reaching the main river you have no option but follow it downstream, although dependent on the state of the tide, the current might actually be flowing upriver. The banks are

Foot of Hardley Flood

thickly cloaked in reeds, so much so, that often the only evidence of the waterway is the tops of the boats gliding by. The river twists sharply past the ruin of the Limpenhoe Drainage Mill on the opposite bank, eventually running to meet the outflow of the River Chet **B**. There, guarded by railings, stands the ancient Hardley Cross, which marks the boundary between the jurisdictions of Yarmouth and Norwich. In years gone by it was the site of an annual ceremony known as the 'Hardley Inquest', when the burghers of the two towns met to declare the 'abuses and privileges' of the trade along the river.

The path turns beside the much narrower Chet, whose convoluted meanderings at first appear to be taking you back to Hardley church. In time, however, the waterway straightens and Hardley Hall comes into view, a substantial brick pile capped with an imposingly high roof. The riverside path continues to the foot of Hardley Flood, which is retained by a low dam **C**. The path lies left along a narrow wooded embankment separating the river from the lake. This is perhaps the most delightful section of the whole walk, with breaks in the reeds and willows

15th-century font in St Margaret's Church

allowing views across the water. Occasional bridges take the path across sluices, which allow the tide to ebb and flow into the lake, thus helping to reduce the risk of flooding upstream. The river is in fact tidal for a further mile upriver, as far as the bridge linking Chedgrave and Loddon. Bird watchers can take advantage of a hide overlooking the Flood towards its far end.

Skirting the edge of Chedgrave Common beyond, the path becomes formalised and is ultimately turned from the river at the edge of a camping site. Joining a lane, follow it up towards the edge of town, turning left just before the end to walk through a children's play area back to the church.

Possibly standing on the site of a Roman encampment (the Roman fort at Burgh is not that far away) the church has ancient origins, which are dramatically stated in the fine early Norman carving of the doorway inside the porch. The church is open during summer afternoons and, inside the vestry, some wall paintings from the 11th century have recently been discovered. ●

SCALE 1:25000 or 2½ INCHES to 1 MILE 4CM to 1KM

walk [13]

🖊 Start

Buck's Common, 1 mile west of Blickling Hall

🎯 Distance

6½ miles (10.5km)

〽 Height gain

195 feet (60m)

🕐 Approximate time

3 hours

🥾 Route terrain

Woodland and field paths, quiet lanes

[P] Parking

National Trust car park

🗺 OS maps

Landranger 133 (North East Norfolk), Explorer 252 (Norfolk Coast East)

📋 GPS waypoints

🖊 TG 155 289
Ⓐ TG 153 293
Ⓑ TG 154 299
Ⓒ TG 161 308
Ⓓ TG 165 305
Ⓔ TG 177 296
Ⓕ TG 175 280

Blickling and the River Bure

The National Trust's Blickling Hall is one of Norfolk's most pleasing country houses and serves as a fine focus for this splendid ramble around its extensive park and the lush water meadows beside the River Bure near Itteringham.

🖊 From the information board at the rear of the car park, keep left with a clear path to parallel the boundary of the wood. After ¼ mile, as it sweeps right, look for a fainter path cutting between the trees to a gap in the perimeter hedge Ⓐ. Joining a hedged track (not the field track just beyond), follow it right, meeting a lane at its end. Go left for 150 yds then, just before the junction, leave through a gap in the hedge opposite a cottage onto the riverside marshes Ⓑ. *If the ongoing path proves too wet, you can retrace your steps to follow the lane in the other direction past Great Wood, rejoining the route as it returns over the River Bure at Ⓓ.*

A path strikes a left diagonal across a lush meadow to a footbridge across the River Bure. Head half-left to another bridge and then turn right. A trod takes the onward way through the marsh down the shallow valley, winding over a succession of bridged drainage ditches. Over the third, bear right as if to follow the river, but when your onward progress is soon barred by a fence, swing left through thicket to find a final pair of bridges on the right. Leaving the wetland meadows behind, the path continues at the edge of grazing pasture. The boundary later curves around towards White House Farm. Exit the final field by a gate just right of a barn and walk up to a track opposite a cottage Ⓒ. Turn right, shortly meeting the end of a lane and go sharp right on a narrowing grass trail. Follow that to a bridge across the Bure and walk out to the lane beyond Ⓓ.

Walk left along the lane for a little over ¼ mile to find a gap in the right-hand bank, shortly before reaching Moorgate Farm. With the hedge on your left, follow a field-edge path towards Blickling's Great Wood. Passing through a gate, keep ahead between the trees and then at the margin of a field. Reaching a junction, go left and at the far side of the field, wind through more trees to a crossway. Keep ahead towards the northern tip of the lake, going as far as the end of the right-hand fence Ⓔ.

Go right to a gate by the water and double back beside the lake, Blickling Hall shortly appearing in view. Keep ahead through a gate, but soon reaching a fence, leave the waterside

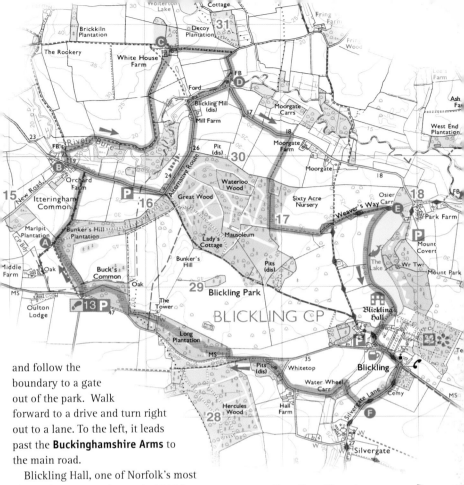

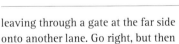

and follow the boundary to a gate out of the park. Walk forward to a drive and turn right out to a lane. To the left, it leads past the **Buckinghamshire Arms** to the main road.

Blickling Hall, one of Norfolk's most elegant houses, was begun in 1616 for Sir Henry Hobart, Lord Chief Justice to James I. It passed to the National Trust in 1940, an important early acquisition.

Turn left to pass the gateway and drive leading to the front of the house. Beyond, St Andrew's Church overlooks the road from a low hill. Turn right just after the church along a narrow lane to Silvergate. Follow it for ¼ mile, but then leave over a waymarked stile through the hedge on the right **F**. A path cuts through a spinney, continuing beside a meadow beyond, along which there is a distant view back to the church. Over more stiles, wind around the edge of another copse, before turning out onto the edge of a field. Follow the perimeter away to the left leaving through a gate at the far side onto another lane. Go right, but then soon bear off left onto a track. Approaching the road, fork off left along a parallel path to meet it further along.

Cross to a track opposite, swinging left into the wood after 20 yds. When it breaks cover, keep ahead past a crenellated brick folly over to the right and continue beside a wood fringed by pine. The ongoing path then delves back into the trees. Following white-topped marker posts, keep left at a junction and then at a crosspath, go left again back to the car park. ●

SCALE 1:27777 or 2¼ INCHES to 1 MILE 3.6CM to 1KM

Start
Fring

Distance
7 miles (11.3km)

Height gain
460 feet (140m)

Approximate time
3½ hours

Route terrain
Country tracks and quiet lanes

Parking
Along lane near All Saints' Church

OS maps
Landranger 132 (North West Norfolk), Explorer 250 (Norfolk Coast West)

GPS waypoints
TF 735 348
Ⓐ TF 727 356
Ⓑ TF 722 368
Ⓒ TF 713 365
Ⓓ TF 739 329
Ⓔ TF 743 328

Peddars Way – Fring and Sedgeford

Although Norfolk is not noted for its uplands, this walk will go a long way to discredit myths hinting at a uniform flatness. The north-west corner is puckered in a gently rolling topography, where widely spaced hills open panoramic views across a bucolic landscape. Combining little-used back lanes and an impressive section of the Peddars Way, this pleasant ramble reveals yet another facet of Norfolk's delightful countryside.

All Saints' at Fring is typical of many Norfolk village churches, where outcrops of solid stone are non-existent and builders had to make the best of the only readily available material, flint. But lack of resources was never an obstacle to true ambition and even in tiny settlements such as this, quite large churches were raised to assert the faith of the community.

The lane north-west from the church falls along the slope of a hill, dropping after some ¾ mile through trees to a bridge at the base of the valley, the site of a Roman ford. Immediately beyond, turn off right onto the Peddars Way Ⓐ. Rising beside a hedge, it tackles the flank of Dove Hill, a modest prominence that just tops 200 feet. After levelling beside a small copse crowning the summit, the path slips through the hedge, descending towards a handful of cottages below. At the bottom of the field, waymarks guide you left and right to a contained path that emerges past the cottages of Littleport onto the main road Ⓑ. Overlooking the road, a short distance to the right, is a rather unusual building, Magazine Cottage.

Having looked at Magazine Cottage, return along the lane, following it past the end of Littleport's cottages towards

Magazine Cottage
Now a private house, the cottage has the appearance more of a chapel than a secular structure and was put up around 1640 by the le Strange family of Old Hunstanton. Staunch supporters of Charles I during the Civil War, they deliberately gave the building an innocuous appearance to disguise its clandestine purpose as an arms store. On the wall are much-weathered shields that once no doubt carried the family crests and from the back roof sprouts an odd dormer, supported by the twin stacks of a tall chimney. Another curious feature is the lean-to extension at the rear, which burrows into the rising hillside.

Sedgeford. Reaching the village, the road bends sharply right in front of a junction at the war memorial **C**. Turn left along the narrow lane signed to

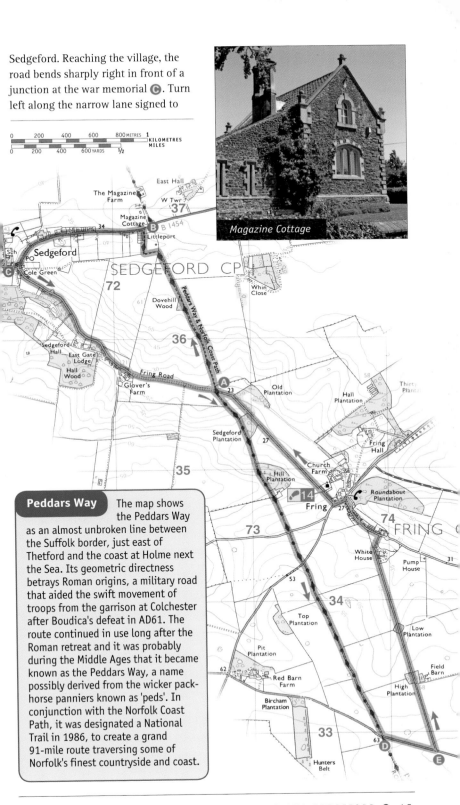

Magazine Cottage

Peddars Way The map shows the Peddars Way as an almost unbroken line between the Suffolk border, just east of Thetford and the coast at Holme next the Sea. Its geometric directness betrays Roman origins, a military road that aided the swift movement of troops from the garrison at Colchester after Boudica's defeat in AD61. The route continued in use long after the Roman retreat and it was probably during the Middle Ages that it became known as the Peddars Way, a name possibly derived from the wicker pack-horse panniers known as 'peds'. In conjunction with the Norfolk Coast Path, it was designated a National Trail in 1986, to create a grand 91-mile route traversing some of Norfolk's finest countryside and coast.

The Norfolk countryside is often gently undulalting

Fring unless you want to detour to the **King William IV** pub, which lies ¼ mile further on. The lane meanders up the valley past the grounds of Sedgeford Hall, later climbing beside a tiny stream ostentatiously christened the Heacham River. Eventually the lane returns you to the point at which you first embarked upon the Peddars Way Ⓐ.

This time, follow it in the other direction above the undulating woods lining the southern slopes of the valley. Beyond a cottage the track becomes a metalled drive, but after crossing a lane reverts to gravel between more open fields. Keep going over a second lane, the way settling on higher ground, where the views encompass the cottages and church at Fring nestling below. Leave the Peddars Way at the third lane

Ⓓ, following it for ¼ mile down the hill. In the middle distance ahead is Bircham Mill, one of Norfolk's few remaining working windmills. Built in 1846, it operated for almost 80 years, but had become derelict by the time restoration began in the late 1970s. Now open to visitors (Apr-Sept), you can climb onto the upper platform, while below afternoon teas feature freshly baked bread and cakes.

Reaching a metalled track Ⓔ, turn off left. It cuts back across the farmed hillside, passing a group of barns and ultimately emerging onto a lane. Walk left into Fring, turning left again towards Shernborne at a three-way junction in the village centre. Then, almost immediately, go right and climb back to the church. ●

Castle Acre and West Acre

Linking two medieval priories and a dramatic castle, this walk wanders beside flood meadows and through a delightful wood bordering the River Nar to West Acre. The return along the hillside above the Nar valley reveals a fine view to Castle Acre's extensive monastic ruins before winding back into the attractive village by way of its impressive fortifications.

walk 15

Start	Castle Acre

Distance	7 miles (11.3km)

Height gain	280 feet (85m)

Approximate time	3½ hours

Route terrain	Field paths, tracks and quiet lanes

Parking	Roadside parking in village

OS maps	Landranger 132 (North West Norfolk), Explorer 236 (King's Lynn, Downham Market & Swaffham)

GPS waypoints

- TF 817 151
- Ⓐ TF 813 150
- Ⓑ TF 780 152
- Ⓒ TF 784 151
- Ⓓ TF 787 137
- Ⓔ TF 800 132

From a junction in front of the Bailey Gate, a long green parallels the High Street, adding another dimension of attractiveness to the picturesque assortment of inns, cottages and houses. Set back at the far end is St James' Church, an interesting building with origins in the 12th century.

St James' Church A doorway in the south wall sits below an earlier, much higher archway, said to have been built to accommodate the entry of knights upon horseback seeking blessing before battle. Simon Jenkins, author of *England's 1000 Best Churches*, suggests it might have been the world's first 'drive in church'. Inside is a magnificent 15th-century font cover, which retains much of its original rich paintwork and gilding. Equally beautiful is the graceful 'wine-glass' pulpit from about the same time, with painted panels and supported on a single, slender pedestal. The lower portion of the rood screen also survives, its panels depicting the twelve apostles.

Continue past the church to a junction at the end of the lane Ⓐ. The onward route lies to the right, but you may first wish to visit the priory.

Castle Acre Priory It was founded by William de Warenne in 1090 as a daughter house to the Cluniac priory he had already established at Lewes in Sussex. The priory lay on one of the pilgrimage routes to Little Walsingham and thus benefited from the trade brought to the area, particularly as it could boast its own relic, the arm of St Philip. Within the extensive precincts were a large number of buildings, many of which can readily be traced amongst the ruins. The west front of the priory church is particularly eye-catching and still stands to the height of the great window above the elaborate doorway.

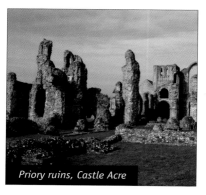

Priory ruins, Castle Acre

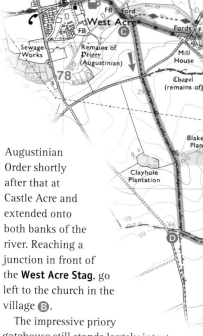

Beyond point **A**, where the lane bends right again, turn off left along Common Road, a track signed as the Nar Valley Way. It falls into the valley, bending to close with the river at the bottom. There, bear off through a kissing-gate on the left, from which a path continues at the edge of riverside marsh. Tall reeds hide all but an occasional glimpse of the river, but there is a fine view across to the woods lining the far bank. Much of the Nar's upper reaches is a designated SSSI, (Site of Special Scientific Interest), the waterside meadows containing a host of flowers such as meadowsweet, once used to flavour mead, and the unusual yellow rattle, which extracts part of its nourishment from the grass roots on which it grows. Later the path enters woodland, undulating through the trees before eventually breaking out at the edge of more open scrub. Keep ahead to a bridge spanning a ditch and carry on to cross the river itself, shortly emerging onto a narrow lane. A path opposite continues across a gorse-covered heath, which sweetens the air with the heady scent of its yellow flowers.

Joining a track, bear right, shortly re-crossing the river. Beyond, there is a view left to the ivy-clad ruins of the church and chapter house of West Acre's priory. It was founded for the Augustinian Order shortly after that at Castle Acre and extended onto both banks of the river. Reaching a junction in front of the **West Acre Stag**, go left to the church in the village **B**.

The impressive priory gatehouse still stands largely intact beside the village church; a splendid 14th-century archway supporting an upper room. Although now roofless, it was inhabited within living memory by an old woman who went in and out via an external staircase. The church itself also has an unusual feature, the hours on the clock face represented by the letters WATCH AND PRAY.

Retrace your steps to the pub and go right, back across the river. Just beyond a subsequent gate, look for a path leaving on the right **C**. The way, contained between a fence and hedge, leads to a narrow lane. Carefully cross to a track opposite, which gently climbs away between open fields, passing a wood halfway up the hill. Stay forward on the main track beside an old outgrown hedge to a junction at the top corner **D**. Turn left and, with a hedge on your left, walk along the spine of the

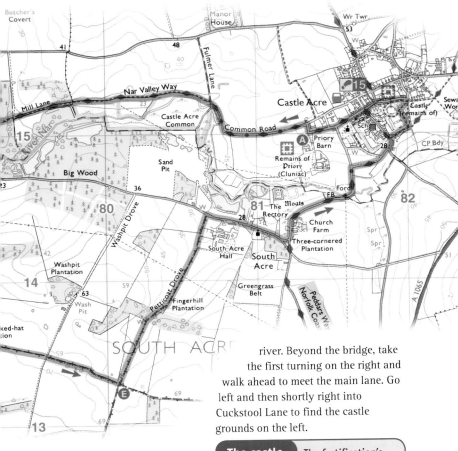

river. Beyond the bridge, take the first turning on the right and walk ahead to meet the main lane. Go left and then shortly right into Cuckstool Lane to find the castle grounds on the left.

The castle

The fortification's earthwork defences are amongst the most impressive in the country, with deep ditches and massive ramparts enclosing an outer bailey, where the village grew, and an inner motte on which stood the central keep. It was built shortly after the Norman Conquest on the site of an existing Saxon settlement by William's son-in-law William de Warenne and his descendants remained there until the blood line died out in the 14th century. Although most of the buildings have succumbed to time, the bailey gate survives more or less intact guarding the road from Swaffham.

hill. The tall hedges and trees provide some shelter from the sometimes unremitting wind, but occasional breaks allow a glimpse to Castle Acre, still a good way off. Keep ahead at a crossway to skirt a small plantation, beyond which, the route meanders down to another junction **E**. To the left, Petticoat Drove falls along a shallow fold in the hillside, passing through more trees before ultimately ending at a lane.

Head right, going by the entrance to South Acre Farm and then the small, flint church of St George. After bearing left at successive junctions, a lovely view soon opens across the valley to the priory before the lane descends to the

After exploring the extensive site, leave behind the motte at the north-west corner, walking out past the village hall. Follow the main street left back into the heart of the village. ●

walk 16

Start
Shotesham

Distance
7 miles (11.3km)

Height gain
245 feet (75m)

Approximate time
3½ hours

Route terrain
Field paths and tracks

Parking
All Saints' Church car park (but not on Sundays or festivals)

OS maps
Landranger 134 (Norwich & The Broads), Explorer 237 (Norwich)

GPS waypoints
- TM 246 990
- Ⓐ TM 245 983
- Ⓑ TM 251 980
- Ⓒ TM 247 972
- Ⓓ TM 246 958
- Ⓔ TM 231 958
- Ⓕ TM 229 970
- Ⓖ TM 230 973
- Ⓗ TM 239 981

Boudica's Way – Shotesham and Saxlingham Nethergate

The walk begins along a stretch of Boudica's Way, which runs from Norwich to Diss and is one of several long-distance paths that explore Norfolk's delightful countryside. Winding between rolling fields, broken by scattered copses and woods, it returns past two abandoned churches and the picturesque village of Saxlingham Nethergate.

A church has stood on the hill above the Beck since Saxon times, looking out across the common, a mile-long stretch of open ground. Through the centre, the stream flows on its way to join the River Tas, along which at one time, boats could sail upriver from Norwich. The village has a curious connection with Greenwich Hospital, founded in 1614 by Henry Howard. Henry's time to enter the world coincided with his mother passing through Shotesham. She was admirably looked after during the birth of her son and on founding the Greenwich Hospital, he repaid the kindness by allowing villagers the right to retire there. In 1879 the hospital trust built an almshouse here so the old folk could remain in their own village.

From the church gate, walk past the war memorial, dropping to meet the end of a track by a bridge. Signed as Boudica's Way to Tasburgh, the track soon shrinks to a path, crosses the brook and delves through trees to emerge on the edge of a field. A cleared path shows the way across, continuing beside the next field to end at a track Ⓐ.

Follow it left and, as it later swings left, keep ahead along a grass margin to the corner of Great Wood. Tacking the perimeter of the trees, eventually pass through a clump of scrub and continue beside a meadow to a gap in the corner Ⓑ. Go right along the eastern edge of the wood. Turn within a corner, but after a few yards, turn right over a planked ditch. Stay with the boundary to the tip of the wood, there moving left to an earth bridge. Head straight down the crop field to meet a lane in front of a small wind turbine Ⓒ.

Go right, but then immediately left at a footpath sign into the field. The path doubles back behind a converted barn, crossing a ditch into the next field. Carry on, the boundary eventually curving right and in due course arriving at a corner in front of trees. Swing right to find a bridge, about 50 yds along and pass through the trees to a lane.

Cross to a track opposite, marked as a footpath, which meanders more or less due south at the field edge, in time reaching Saxlingham Grove, a private wood. Turn right to the corner of the wood ⓓ and go right again, walking away with the hedge on your left. Carry on from field to field until faced with more trees. Again turn right and, at the next corner, go left across the ditch, following the boundary of the copse out to a lane.

Some 50 yds to the left, a footpath leaves on the opposite side. Towards the

Ruins of St Mary's Church

St Mary's Church

The earliest parts of the ruined church date to around 1100, all that is left of the tiny village of Saxlingham Thorpe. Here on the hill, the settlement was exposed to the worst of the wind and rain and, over time, the population drifted to the shelter of the valley. In 1573, the church was attached to the rector of Saxlingham Nethergate, an indication of dwindling congregations but by the 1680s had been abandoned, its stone being taken for repairs at Nethergate.

junction. Go right to emerge in the centre of Saxlingham Nethergate by the war memorial ⑤. Follow the main lane right to find the church, set back above a small green on the left. Enter the churchyard and pass below the tower, which carries both a one-fingered clock and a sundial. Samuel King, rector in 1851, was an amateur geologist and a friend and occasional assistant of Sir Charles Lyell, who rightly perceived that the world was being shaped by ongoing forces and not just cataclysmic events.

Leave through a gate at the north-western corner and head away at the field edge, passing out in the corner to find a stile on the right ⑥. Over that, turn right and walk the length of a mead. Negotiating a stile at the end, move right to continue forward along an unploughed strip, eventually emerging at the corner of a lane. Follow it ahead and then left over a bridge, ignoring the lane off to the right. Some 100 yds after passing a cottage on the right, leave through a gap in the right-hand hedge ⑦. Follow the boundary away from the road, but after 200 yds, by a power-cable post, bear left across the field, coming out at the far side opposite a junction of lanes. Take the one ahead, signed to Stoke Cross, which climbs past the ivy-clad ruins of St Martin's Church. Take a path just beyond to its neighbour, St Mary's, pass through the churchyard to the north-east corner and walk on at the field edge. A stile by an old oak half-way along marks the point at which you then turn right, now making for the church at Shotesham. Cross an intervening lane to continue in the next field, swinging right and then left around the corner of a spinney. Meeting another lane, turn right and, at the bottom, go left back to the church. ●

far end of the second field, walk past a wooded track signed off left, Pymar's Lane, but reaching the corner ④, turn right, remaining within the field. At the bottom, drop to a three-fingered signpost at the base of a gully. Climb ahead along an enclosed way, the bounding hedgerows displaying a succession of flowers throughout spring and summer. Crossing a gravel track, keep forward through a strip of wood. Breaking out at the end, go ahead and then bear left on a contained path beside another copse, which conceals the roofless ruin of a church.

At the corner, turn right, the path soon curving with the field edge to a

Thompson Common and the Pingos

'Pingo', an Inuit word meaning 'small hill', excites the imagination and this intriguing trail does just that, leading you through dense carr (marshy woodland) past any number of, not hillocks, but mysterious pools. The route continues along a Roman road and through forest before returning on an exceptionally pretty stretch of former railway line.

walk 17

Start
Northern end of the Great Eastern Pingo Trail

Distance
7 miles (11.3km)

Height gain
Negligible

Approximate time
3½ hours

Route terrain
Country tracks and woodland paths

Parking
Car park beside A1075, 3 miles south of Watton

Dog friendly
Dogs are not allowed on Thompson Common

OS maps
Landranger 144 (Thetford & Diss), Explorers 237 (Norwich) or 229 (Thetford in The Brecks)

GPS waypoints
TL 940 965
Ⓐ TL 933 966
Ⓑ TL 925 953
Ⓒ TL 913 948
Ⓓ TL 920 932
Ⓔ TL 925 936
Ⓕ TL 927 931

> ### Pingos
>
> Pingos are a relic of the last Ice Age, the result of successive freeze and thaw of pockets of underground spring water, which pushed the overlying earth into ringed mounds of debris. When the climate finally warmed, the permafrost melted and the hillocks collapsed leaving lipped craters, which filled with water to give the pools we see today. Around the Thompson Common Nature Reserve, the pingos are some of the best examples in Britain, scattered throughout a thick carr supporting an outstanding array of plant and wildlife. Flowers such as water violet and bog-bean grow in the ponds and trees sprout out of living islands of greater tussock sedge. Coots dabble around the fringes and dragonflies and butterflies are the most colourful of the multitude of insects you will find here.

The car park occupies the site of the former Stow Bedon Station and lies behind a lay-by off the main road. The walk starts from a concealed exit opposite its entrance. Pass into the trees and through a kissing-gate to follow a winding path through the close woodland of Thompson Common, passing a succession of primeval-looking pingos. Breaking out into more open ground, keep on between two pools, in time reaching a waymark by a kissing-gate. Passing back into thicket, the path meanders by more dark ponds before emerging onto a lane Ⓐ.

Go left, continuing beyond its end on a cart track. Where that too eventually turns away, keep ahead on a path that in due course leads to a gate. Follow a trod across open meadow to a kissing-gate at the far corner Ⓑ. Cross a stream back into the wood, the ongoing path hugging the ditch bank and ultimately reaching a crossing track. Swing right, re-crossing the stream and walk on for 100 yds before branching left by a waymark. Fork left again at a later junction, passing more pingos and a hide that looks out from the reeds at the tip of

A pingo pond

Thompson Water. It is an artificial lake created in the mid 19th century and attracts many birds such as reed warblers, great crested grebe and water rail. The way finally leaves the nature reserve through a kissing-gate by an information board and car park **C**.

Walk forward along the access drive to meet the Peddars Way and follow that left past the foot of the lake. There follows a very pleasant walk of over a mile, during which the bordering scenery varies between woodland, forest, heath grazing and pasture. Where the fence bounding the military area finally ends, look for a fingerpost indicating a footpath off into the wood on the left **D**. Turn in through the trees and continue at the perimeter of replanted pine and birch, which contrasts with the delightful mixture of trees in the old wood on your left. Towards the top end of the plantation, the path swings around to the right **E**.

A broad grass track heads towards a stand of mature pine. Fork left into the trees, keeping ahead at the far side. Shortly reaching another junction bear left and immediately go left again through a wooden barrier **F**.

You are now following the track bed of the former Thetford and Swaffham Railway, which opened in 1869 and was later absorbed within the Great Eastern network. The line finally closed in 1965 as part of the rationalisation programme,

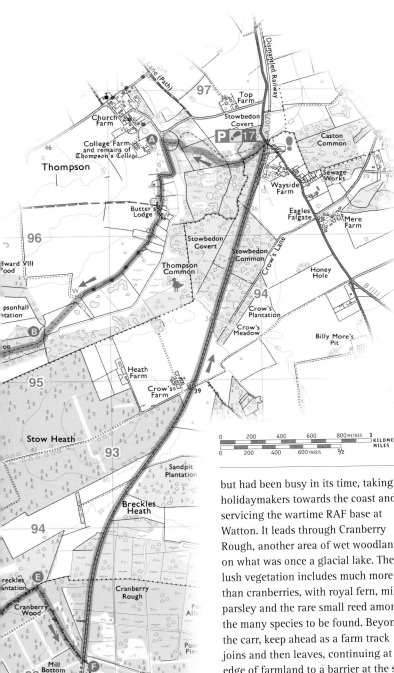

SCALE 1:25000 or 2½ INCHES to 1 MILE 4CM to 1KM

but had been busy in its time, taking holidaymakers towards the coast and servicing the wartime RAF base at Watton. It leads through Cranberry Rough, another area of wet woodland on what was once a glacial lake. The lush vegetation includes much more than cranberries, with royal fern, milk parsley and the rare small reed amongst the many species to be found. Beyond the carr, keep ahead as a farm track joins and then leaves, continuing at the edge of farmland to a barrier at the site of a crossing keeper's cottage. Go over a gravel track and carry on along a tree-lined trail, which ultimately returns you behind a farm to the car park by the old station yard.

●

Westwick Woods and the Weavers' Way

Start
North Walsham

Distance
7 miles (11.3km)

Height gain
215 feet (65m)

Approximate time
3½ hours

Route terrain
Country tracks and field paths

P Parking
Weavers' Way car park off Station Road

OS maps
Landranger 133 (North East Norfolk), Explorer 252 (Norfolk Coast East)

GPS waypoints
TG 275 300
Ⓐ TG 269 295
Ⓑ TG 270 284
Ⓒ TG 265 267
Ⓓ TG 265 262
Ⓔ TG 254 259
Ⓕ TG 257 268
Ⓖ TG 251 287

North Walsham is a bustling market town and former railway junction. Although the main route from Norwich survives, the two local lines have long gone and the Aylsham branch now forms part of the Weavers' Way. This serves as the return for a charming walk which heads out through Westwick Woods to the tiny hamlet of Swanton Abbott.

Motorists will begin the walk from the Weavers' Way car park on Station Road, west of the town, *but you can arrive at North Walsham by train. If that is the case, leave the station and cross Norwich Road to Station Road opposite. Walk away from the town centre for a little over ¼ mile, bearing right at a mini-roundabout to find the parking area on the left.* Exit the rear of the car park onto the former railway line and follow it to the right, before long reaching a lane, Tungate Road Ⓐ.

Turn left past a junction and Wayside Farm then, as the road bends just beyond, bear left onto a bridleway, marked on the map as Drift Lane. It curves between fields towards the corner of Lord Anson's Wood, there turning to run within the fringe of trees. Breaking out at the edge of an open field, walk on to turn within the shallow corner.

At the next corner Ⓑ keep ahead across the expansive field to a stile at the far side. Diagonally opposite, a track delves into the splendid woodland of North Walsham Heath, a fine mix of mature trees including beech, sweet chestnut, oak and holly. Passing the abandoned farmstead of Strawberry Hall, keep ahead on the track, which continues beside a hedge at the edge of the plantation for almost a further ¾ mile. Eventually, pass through a gate and a final belt of trees to emerge onto a lane at Swanton Abbott Ⓒ.

Go right, but after 75 yds turn off along a track, marked as a footpath, passing between the cottages on the left. It soon narrows to a hedged path amongst the fields, leading to a lane at the entrance of the square-towered St Michael's Church Ⓓ.

Follow Youngmans Lane to the right, which, past the school degenerates to a path. It leads more or less in a straight line at the edge of successive fields, eventually cutting across the middle of an arable field to a gap at the far side Ⓔ. Through that, swing right beside the hedge, but where the boundary later

St Michael's Church

The present building dates from the 12th century, but replaces a Saxon church mentioned in a document of 1044. It refers to it being gifted to St Benet's Abbey, which explains the distinguishing suffix of 'Abbott' to the village's name. St Michael's treasure is a fine brass of the Reverend Stephen Multon, the 15th-century rector of the church, whose initials appear on the screen which commemorated the completion of the chancel. Its painted panels depict the twelve apostles, which, although damaged, remain clear enough to be identified.

turns away, keep ahead across two final fields to join a lane. Go right passing

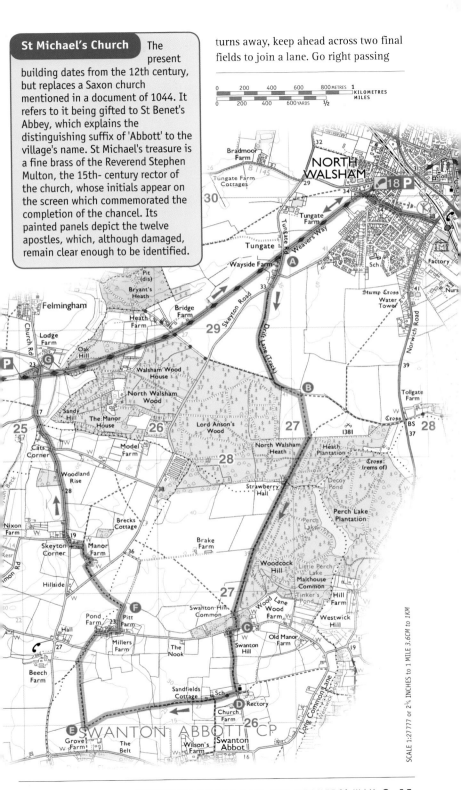

Pond Farm and then turn left towards North Walsham. After 200 yds, leave through a signed opening in the left-hand hedge **F**.

Strike to a lane at the far side and keep going along the track in front, down to Manor Farm. Waymarks guide you right and left through the yard and past barns, the ongoing track leading to a house and swinging left to another lane at Skeyton Corner. Heading right and ignoring side roads, walk on for ¾ mile, eventually dipping beneath a bridge. Leave immediately beyond, turning left **G** to a small parking area. Walk through to rejoin the line of the North Walsham Railway, doubling back left again to follow it past the platform and waiting room of the former Felmingham Station. The track runs pleasantly on as the Weavers' Way, passing through a corner of North Walsham Wood and then between more open fields. It eventually re-crosses Tungate Road and returns to the car park.

Although only railway travellers need continue into the town, others will find the short additional excursion worthwhile.

North Walsham The town grew to prominence in the Middle Ages as a focus for the weaving trade and has a number of attractive buildings in the old centre. Horatio Nelson undertook his education at the grammar school and there is an imposing covered 16th-century market cross in the square, where a lively Thursday market still takes place. Behind is the large church, devoid of its tower, which partly succumbed to a storm in 1724 before falling completely 100 years later. Inside is a lofty, carved font cover, which dates from the middle of the 15th century.

Gentle countryside around North Walsham

West Runton and Beacon Hill

Norfolk is not known for its hills, but its celebrated high point is Beacon Hill overlooking West Runton. This grand walk onto its summit exploits the fine views, but begins along a splendid beach backed by high cliffs of crumbling clay and chalk that have given up some remarkable fossils.

⚠ The 2½-mile beach between East Runton and Sheringham can become impassible at high tide, with intermediate escape only possible at West Runton and Beeston Regis. Consult tide tables (posted by the car park) before setting off.

🖊 Go down to the beach and, negotiating successive low groynes, walk west, the easiest walking being on the sand revealed by the ebbing tide. At West Runton Gap (an exit if necessary), cross a low break in the high groyne, beyond which the beach's character abruptly alters. Seaweed-smothered flint nodules litter the lower beach and a chalk pavement towards the head now offers the best passage. Farther along, a wooden staircase provides a second escape, but otherwise continue to Sheringham, where steps rise onto the promenade **Ⓐ**.

West Runton cliffs

Much of Norfolk's coast is low-lying and backed by sand dunes, shingle bank or salt marsh, but in this north-east corner, it rises into a formidable line of cliffs footed on chalk and overlain by glacial clays. Embedded within the chalk are bands of flint nodules, which, being harder, remain as it is worn away. Just beyond West Runton Gap are curious formations known as paramoudras or potstones, whose formation has yet to be explained. Doughnut-shaped nodules, some looking like fossilised vertebrae are plentifully scattered about, while some much larger rings lie embedded in the chalk. Just east of the high groyne, a dark deposit at the cliff base is rich in fossils. The most spectacular find was in 1990, when the pelvic bone of a giant mammoth was revealed. Subsequent excavation recovered an almost-complete skeleton, parts of which are displayed at museums in Cromer and Norwich. Known as the West Runton Elephant, it weighed over 10 tons and, aside from the dinosaurs, is the largest land creature yet discovered.

---

walk 19

🏁 Start
East Runton

🚩 Distance
7¼ miles (11.7km)

⛰ Height gain
575 feet (175m)

🕐 Approximate time
3½ hours

👟 Route terrain
Field and woodland paths, rocky beach. Note: consult tide tables before setting off

🅿 Parking
East Runton Beach car park (pay and display)

🧭 OS maps
Landranger 133 (North East Norfolk), Explorer 252 (Norfolk Coast East)

📟 GPS waypoints

🖊 TG 200 427
Ⓐ TG 162 435
Ⓑ TG 171 427
Ⓒ TG 170 417
Ⓓ TG 183 414
Ⓔ TG 189 424

Climb the drive from the top of the steps and go left beside a putting green to join the coast path onto Beeston Bump. One of Norfolk's highest coastal points and manned as a lookout during the last war, it offers a grand view. Continue downhill to the edge of a caravan park and turn from the coast. Cautiously cross the railway line and follow a track to the main road **B**.

Cross left to a drive and then go right, passing Hall Farm and a campsite. A track continues towards Beeston Regis Heath. At a junction with Calves Well Lane, go right, skirting a cottage to continue along a hedged track. Ignore a broad grass trail to the left, instead taking a lesser path farther along. Climb along a wooded fold onto the heath and keep right, soon reaching a splendid cairned viewpoint **C**.

Retrace your steps to a fork and bear right to a fence in the trees. Follow it

East Runton Beach

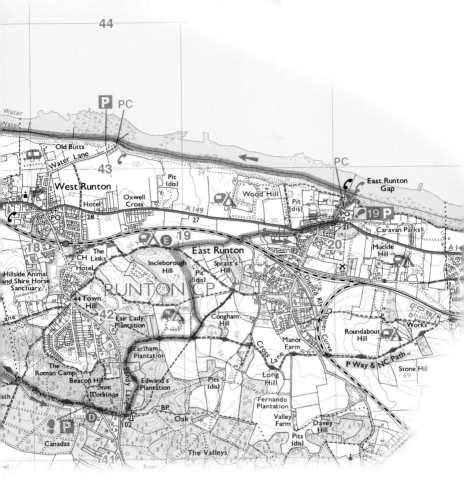

| 0 | 200 | 400 | 600 | 800 METRES | 1 |
| 0 | 200 | 400 | 600 YARDS | ½ | |

KILOMETRES
MILES

left to a junction at its corner. Walk ahead on a narrow path, keeping left where it then splits. A clear path runs through the wood for nearly ½ mile to a crosspath. There, move left to find a broader track. The route lies to the right, but you might first wander from the trees to enjoy the view.

After ¼ mile, the track passes a small National Trust car park at the high point of Beacon Hill, beside which are distinctive earthworks, the 'Roman Camp' **D**. Although the embankments are old, their Roman association is a Victorian fantasy to embellish a local beauty spot with a hint of mystery. The hill however was an excellent viewpoint and a signal beacon is known to have existed from the 14th century.

Follow the drive to a lane and cross to the track opposite. Fork left to West Runton Camping and Caravanning Club Site, where light refreshments are available. Continue past the entrance to a 4-way junction and turn left, watching for a stile on the left at the edge of the trees. Over this, head to another stile at the end of the path and walk along a meadow, leaving towards its far end over a stile on the right onto a track **E**. Go right and then fork left. Cross a bridge spanning the railway and follow the track to the road. Walk right, into East Runton, turning left back to the beach car park. ●

Wiveton Downs and Cley next the Sea

Start

Wiveton Downs

Distance

7¾ miles (12.5km)

Height gain

215 feet (65m)

Approximate time

3½ hours

Route terrain

Coast and field paths

Parking

Car park at Wiveton Downs

OS maps

Landranger 133 (North East Norfolk), Explorer 251 (Norfolk Coast Central)

GPS waypoints

    TG 030 422
Ⓐ TG 042 427
Ⓑ TG 048 431
Ⓒ TG 045 439
Ⓓ TG 043 441
Ⓔ TG 026 440
Ⓕ TG 016 440
Ⓖ TG 023 432

The north Norfolk coast is a remarkable melding of shifting sand and marsh, an uncertain and vague boundary between land and sea. Nowhere is that no-man's-land better illustrated than around Blakeney and Cley next the Sea, where old trading ports are now well distanced from the open waters. The walk begins among the low hills behind, deposited beneath glacial sheets as the last Ice Age drew to a close.

A pleasant lane with broad verges leads downhill from the car park entrance to a junction and open green below Wiveton church Ⓐ. It was built in the early part of the 15th century to serve a small, but busy fishing and trading port. There is a reminder of those times in the upturned canon planted on the green and also in images of ships inscribed on stones within the church. Interesting features include a massive parish chest with five separate locks.

Take the lane that runs to the right of the church, which crosses the River Glaven on its way to Cley by the ancient Wiveton Bridge. Still following signs to Cley go left, soon reaching a much larger green overlooked by St Margaret's Church Ⓑ. Its almost cathedral-like proportions and elaborate decoration reflect the wealth brought to the village by medieval trade with the Hanseatic ports. Walk through the graveyard below the foot of the tower, leaving through a gate near the north-west corner from which a track leads out to a back lane. Go left, keeping ahead beyond the entrance to Cley Hall to its very end. Dog-leg right and left into a narrow, almost tunnel-like ginnel that drops between unseen gardens to emerge onto the main road Ⓒ.

During the 17th century, passage upriver to the harbour near the church became increasingly difficult because of silting and, after a disastrous fire that destroyed many of the houses, it was decided to rebuild the village at its present location nearer the sea. A charmingly haphazard assortment of cottages and houses evolved, the most prominent building being the windmill, which lies down a track on the right.

Follow the main road left as it twists left and right through the village, climbing onto a raised path immediately beyond the last of the cottages. After crossing the River Glaven, follow the Peddars Way and Norfolk Coast Path right, carried along the top of a dike above the marshes. There is a fine view

SCALE 1:25000 or 2½ INCHES to 1 MILE 4CM to 1KM

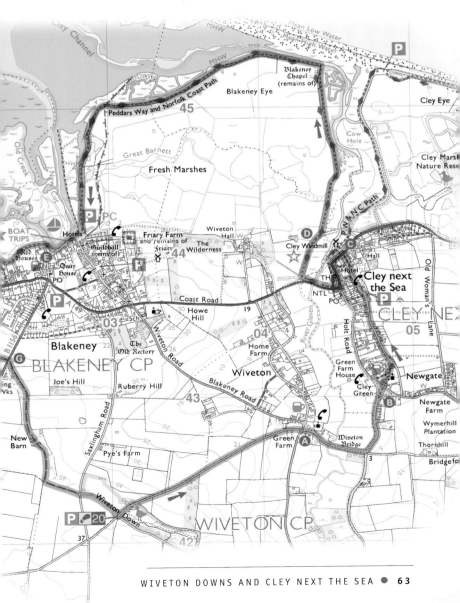

Cley windmill

Following the crest of a grassy wall at the edge of the salt marshes, it passes the long allotment gardens backing the old fishermen's houses and then a succession of fields. After ½ mile, approaching a higher dike, turn left onto a path climbing away beside a hedge **F**.

Emerging onto the coast road at the edge of the village, go right. After 50 yds, bear left at a footpath sign into the corner of a field. Keep left around the base of a gorse-covered hill and, in the next field, turn right beside a hedge. At the top of the field, go left into a corner and then wind right through a belt of trees. Turn left beside the perimeter of Kettle Hill Plantation, swinging left again around the corner. Eventually meeting a drive, follow it right out to a lane **G**.

A bridleway sign opposite marks the beginning of a grass track that rises past the gorse-covered mounds and hollows of old gravel pits. Passing a farm at the top of the hill, keep ahead on its access track that leads down to another lane. Cross to the left-hand one of the pair of gates facing you from which a path meanders between more workings on Wiveton Downs, taking you back to the car park entrance. ●

across reed beds back to the village, a motley collection of black and orange tiled roofs dominated by the 18th-century windmill, while the reed beds themselves are harvested for use as thatching. As the way draws opposite the old quayside by the windmill, drop left to a lower embankment **D**, which continues parallel with the river towards the sea. Even this slight elevation brings a significant head-and-shoulders advantage, opening a grand panorama along the coastline in both directions. The sea, however, remains hidden from view by a high outer bank, still far in the distance. Eventually, the river channel curves to the left and begins to widen behind the outer sea wall. Before long the path turns again beside another creek, heading inland once more towards Blakeney. Reaching the village, turn right along the harbour road, passing the entrance to the Guildhall (English Heritage) and the High Street where you will find refreshment.

At the far end of the harbour, the coast path is signed off on the right **E**.

> ### Blakeney Esker
> Wiveton Downs is part of a glacial feature known as Blakeney Esker, a prominent ridge of sand and gravels that was laid down by a melt-water river running in tunnels beneath an overlying ice sheet. The unconsolidated ground made exploitation easy and from prehistoric times the area has been periodically quarried for nodules of flint. The scrub and grassland on the down is now a haven for wildlife and attracts many birds such as woodcock, short eared owl, linnet and yellowhammer.

The Burnhams

Seven separate parishes once all answered to 'Burnham' in this corner of Norfolk. The ramble includes just four of the villages, each with its own distinctive character and incorporates a bracing stretch along the coast overlooking the estuary of the River Burn.

> **The Burnhams** Burnham Market is the largest of the group, its attractive houses and shops divided by a spacious central green. It grew as the hub of the community and overlooked the River Burn, along which trade was conducted via the port at Burnham Overy Town. The river became un-navigable in the Middle Ages and a new harbour was built at Burnham Overy Staithe. Nearby Burnham Thorpe is perhaps the most famous of the scattered settlements, being the birthplace of Britain's greatest admiral, Horatio Nelson, whose father was parson there. His inspiration no doubt stemmed from watching boats at Burnham Staithe as a boy.

From the war memorial in Burnham Market (at the opposite end of the green from the church), cross the road and leave the town along Herrings Lane. Beyond the last of the houses, continue over the hill to a bend, there finding a signpost marking a path through a hole in the hedge on the left towards Burnham Norton. Follow the field edge to the bottom, joining a track that leads out to the road. Keep ahead along the lane opposite, which goes into Burnham Norton. At the far end of the hamlet, where the lane swings sharply left, turn off along a track on the right **Ⓐ**.

Beyond the back of a building, the track bends left through a cattle pen to continue between reed-bound ditches across the grazing marsh. The marshes attract many birds particularly in winter. The marsh harrier nests here as do other birds, including water rail, bearded tit and reed warbler. Reaching a pair of gates, mount a stile beside the right-hand one and carry on along a grass track to the sea wall, crossing a bridged ditch at the end to gain the embankment **Ⓑ**.

To the right, the Coast Path winds around the patches of grazing separated, not by hedges, but ditches. On the other hand stretches the sea marsh, fragmented by muddy channels that flood with the rising tide. Ahead is Burnham Overy Staithe, the next village on the route, but as it becomes tantalisingly close the channel of the River Burn frustratingly

Sidebar

Start
Burnham Market

Distance
7½ miles (12.1km)

Height gain
230 feet (70m)

Approximate time
3½ hours

Route terrain
Coast and field paths, quiet lanes

Parking
Roadside parking in Burnham Market

OS maps
Landranger 132 (North West Norfolk), Explorer 251 (Norfolk Coast Central)

GPS waypoints
- TF 832 421
- Ⓐ TF 828 441
- Ⓑ TF 834 452
- Ⓒ TF 837 438
- Ⓓ TF 853 448
- Ⓔ TF 842 428

Pleasure boats on Overy Creek

turns the bank away. It is only upstream that a bridge takes the way across, the path then dropping off the embankment and bearing left across a field towards the road in front of Burnham Overy Windmill ⒞.

Built in 1816, the mill operated for over a century before being converted to holiday homes in 1926, a practice continued by the National Trust, to whom it now belongs. Close by (conveniently reached by a field path over a stile on the right just after crossing the River Burn) is a picturesque watermill overlooking a pool beside the road. Known as the 'Lower Mill' to distinguish it from the 'Union Mill' passed a little later in the walk, it dates from 1790. Later converted to steam, the mill worked until 1939. It was badly damaged by fire in 1959, and then largely restored by the National Trust.

Head left to the village, initially avoiding the road along a path within the field edge. Go left at the first junction down to the harbour. With so many mills in the area, it is hardly surprising that the main trade was based upon grain, some of it being malted for the production of beer. The former warehouses and maltings still overlook the port, although now converted for other uses. Where the road turns away at the eastern end of the quay, keep forward on a raised path above the car park. Through a gate swing left and continue along the embankment above Overy Creek, which later bends right and then abruptly left. Leave at that point, dropping to a gate below ⒟.

A grass track heads across the fields, eventually rising between high hedges to meet the main road. Continue along the narrow lane opposite that climbs onto a low hill. At the crest, through a broad, signed gap on the right, walk away with the hedge on your left, looking for a waymark about 150 yds along. Pass through an opening and cut diagonally across the corner of the adjacent field to a break in the end hedge. Maintain your direction across the next large field, emerging at a byway. Go left but immediately turn right onto a hedged grass track that ends by an uneven terrace of cottages. Turn left to a junction in Burnham Overy Town ⒠.

The nail stone On the tiny green in the centre of the village is a 'nail' stone over which merchants clinched their deals, a practice that gave rise to the expression 'paying on the nail'.

Carry on along the road ahead towards Burnham Market, which shortly sweeps around across the river in front of the Union Mill. It is unusual in that the waterwheel and adjacent windmill were coupled and power to drive the stones could be taken from either source. It is one of only two mills in Norfolk where this arrangement was used. The complex was built in 1737 and still working in the middle of the

20th century, despite the windmill tower suffering a disastrous fire in 1935.

Reaching the edge of town turn off right into Friars Lane, walking along to the school, opposite which are the remains of a Carmelite friary. The first in Norfolk, it was established around 1245 after the friars were driven from the Holy Land.

The onward way leaves on the left just before the school, signed to Norton Church, a narrow path cutting through to another quiet lane. Turn right up to St Margaret's which has a most beautiful 'wine-glass' pulpit, its painted panels representing the four doctors of the Church: Ambrose, Augustine, Jerome and Gregory. Leave the lane on a track beside the churchyard gate, which leads you back to Herrings Lane. Retrace your outward steps to Burnham Market.   ●

Longer walks of 4 hours and over

Howard's Drainage Mill

Denver Sluice – a three rivers walk

walk 22

Start
Fordham

Distance
8½ miles (13.7km)

Height gain
Negligible

Approximate time
4 hours

Route terrain
Riverside and field paths

Parking
Riverside parking area

OS maps
Landranger 143 (Ely & Wisbech), Explorer 228 (March & Ely)

GPS waypoints
🖊 TL 614 995
Ⓐ TL 619 987
Ⓑ TF 589 009
Ⓒ TF 595 000
Ⓓ TL 588 995
Ⓔ TL 596 989

Until the 17th century, Norfolk's western boundary was a vast marshland fed by the rivers Nene and Great Ouse. Ambitious drainage schemes transformed it into rich farmland, kept viable by an intricate network of channels, ditches and pumps. The best place to appreciate the mammoth scale of the undertaking is Denver Sluice, where several outflows come together.

🖊 Take the track from the parking area towards a bridge spanning the Cut-Off Channel, which runs from the River Lark at Mildenhall, some 20 miles south east. Immediately before the bridge, drop left to a riverside path and head upstream. Climb onto the main A10 road at the next bridge and cross the water, passing a road off to Hilgay. Leave just before yet another bridge, descending right onto the bank of the River Wissey Ⓐ.

Stride away on a pleasant path beside the meandering river, a favourite stretch with boat owners who enjoy its backwater atmosphere. Beyond Khartoum Wood, the river passes beneath a low railway bridge, the footpath dipping to the side. Regain the raised bank and carry on beside the river to the River Great Ouse. Much wider and following a straighter course than its tributary, it continues towards Denver Sluice, where tall gantries carrying drop locks tower above the water. Over to the left runs a high embankment containing the New Bedford River or Hundred Foot Drain, whilst to the right, another embankment hides the Cut-Off Channel along which the walk began. Approaching Denver Sluice, the path passes through a gate and along an avenue of poplar to another gate at the end of a metalled service drive Ⓑ.

Keep along the drive ahead, which crosses the diversion sluice then swings right across the Cut-Off Channel. Before reaching the lane, turn left on a permissive footpath, which cuts through to the road bridge. Re-cross the Cut-Off Channel and then the Relief Channel, following the road around past a car park to the River Great Ouse itself, just above the point at which it merges with the New Bedford River. The **Jenyns Arms** is just a little farther on.

Retrace your steps to Ⓑ, passing through the gate at the end of the tarmac drive.

Until the 17th century, the waterlogged fens provided a rich resource for the folk settled on the higher ground. Fish, waterfowl and eggs supplemented the diet, willows and reeds were used for baskets and thatching and lush meadows gave summer grazing and winter hay. But enterprising landowners saw greater profits in farming the rich peaty soil and in 1650 employed Dutch engineers to banish the waters. Despite the fenmen's objections, ambitious schemes to straighten rivers and build sluices began changing the face of the landscape. But, success was short-lived, for the drying ground caused the peat to shrink, thus dropping the fields below sea level. The more effective the drainage, the lower the land fell, and within 50 years uncontrollable flooding brought them back to square one.

Despite ever-higher embankments and more powerful pumps, today's rising sea levels further exacerbate the situation - a never-ending and unwinnable battle.

The Denver lock controls water flow to the sea but also allows navigation into the upper river system. The original lock was built by the Dutch engineer, Vermuyden in 1651 and allowed passage only when the water levels equalised. Subsequent improvements culminated in a design by the great canal engineer John Rennie in 1834, which enabled boats to pass at all stages of the tide and his lock remains substantially as it was built.

A concessionary path, leaving left, follows a grass track that winds around the end of a field to gain the embankment above the Cut-Off Channel. *(However, if the concessionary path is subsequently closed, simply continue beside the Rivers Great Ouse and Wissey, retracing your steps under the railway bridge.)* Reaching the railway

C, drop right to a stile and head away beside the track. After almost ¼ mile, the dike swings right, continuing between fields of different levels to meet the River Great Ouse **D**. Retrace your outward route beside the River Wissey and beneath the railway bridge.

Some places have too much water, but others too little. And although the Cut-Off Channel was built to drain the land into the sea, water shortage in the

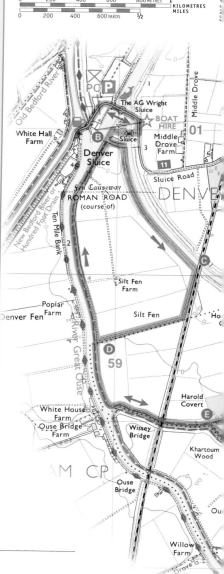

The moorings at Denver Sluice

South East spawned a scheme to reverse its flow and pump water through a pipeline over the hills to top-up Essex reservoirs.

Carry on for a further 300 yds but then, at a bend in the river, drop off the embankment to a gate **E**. Walk away on a track, initially beside a wood, and keep ahead between open fields to a junction by a farm. Go forward, the track eventually curving beside a poplar-lined embankment. Soon, a break allows the passage of the Catchwater Drain to the river and *you can either remain with the ongoing track or slip through onto a fishermen's path along the bank.* Either way, you will shortly reach a bridge that takes you back across the river to the parking area.

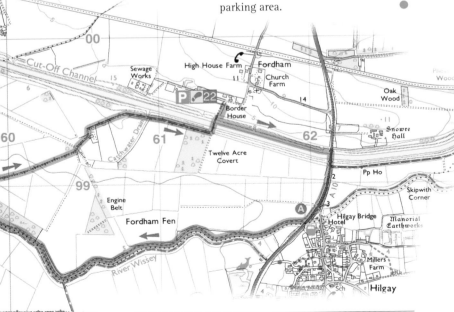

walk 23

Start

Wells-next-the-sea, from the harbour

Distance

8½ miles (13.7km)

Height gain

330 feet (100m)

Approximate time

4 hours

Route terrain

Coastal paths, tracks and country lanes

Parking

Harbour car park (pay and display)

OS maps

Landranger 132 (North West Norfolk), Explorer 251 (Norfolk Coast Central)

GPS waypoints

TF 915 438
Ⓐ TF 922 437
Ⓑ TF 948 438
Ⓒ TF 937 401
Ⓓ TF 915 413

Wells-next-the-Sea, Warham and Wighton

Coastal marshes and rolling countryside are contrasted in this admirable circuit of paths and quiet lanes, which begins from the attractive town of Wells-next-the-Sea and includes a couple of farming villages, each with a country pub. The Norfolk coastal resorts are very popular during summer and Wells is no exception, when parking may be a problem. Considerate roadside parking at Wighton offers an alternative start point.

Wells-next-the-Sea   The Trade Description's Act was not on the Statutes when the Town Council formally adopted Wells-next-the-Sea for its name in 1956, which was perhaps fortunate, since the sea was, even then, over a mile away. That has not always been the case and a channel once came inland as far as the church. Wells developed as a substantial medieval port for the export of grain, which together with malting was an important industry right through into the 20th century. Its heyday was during the 19th century, when the quayside was built, with cargo ships coming and going on almost every tide. Although business declined after the arrival of the railway, occasional small traders have passed through within the last 50 years. Fishing too was important and there is still a small fleet sailing from the harbour. The town has had a lifeboat since 1869, originally sited in the Old Lifeboat House, but relocated 26 years later to its present station at the harbour entrance. The Old Lifeboat House is now a maritime museum.

From the Old Lifeboat House, walk east along the quayside, passing the massive granary and loading gantry, built around 1905 and now converted into apartments. Where the main road then turns away, keep ahead past sea-front cottages and the sailing club headquarters. At the end of the street Ⓐ, carry on beside the old whelk sheds and a boatyard on a track signed as the Norfolk Coast Path to Stiffkey. Quitting the town, it runs along the flood defences above a tidal channel, where the disintegrating ribs of boats' corpses lie half-buried in the mud. The coast path continues, briefly detouring around the head of a creek since a long-ago storm reduced the bridge to a line of stunted posts. After passing through thicket, the way carries on at the edge of the seemingly endless salt marsh and snaking muddy rivulets, which stretch for almost a mile to the north. Ignore the first obvious track off right, Garden Drove, and continue for a further ⅓ mile to a gate marking the end of Cocklestrand Drove **B**.

Follow a hedged dirt track away from the coast to the main A149 road. Cross to the narrow lane opposite, which leads on towards Warham. At a junction in the village beside the **Three Horseshoes**, again go straight over. Climb the ongoing lane past All Saints' Church, the way now signed to Wighton. At the top of the hill, a track leads off right to an Iceni ring fort known as Warham Camp.

Carry on along the lane to a junction at the bottom of the hill and turn right into Wighton. Walk through the village past the **Carpenters Arms**, bending right just beyond. Ignore a lane off to the church and, at the top of the village, keep right towards Wells. However, as the road then immediately bends, abandon it for the by-road that continues straight ahead **C**.

After crossing a bridge over the Wells-Walsingham miniature railway, it runs as an undulating flint track between the fields and eventually rises through a wood to a junction on Gallow Hill by a pretty Victorian cottage **D**. Take the second right, which is signed as a cycleway to Wells and Holkham and gently descends giving a fine panorama to the coast. Lower down, where the main track swings to the

> **Warham Camp** Sited on the flank rather than the summit of the hill, its defences were enhanced by an encircling bend in the River Stiffkey. It appears to have been occupied for around 300 years from about 200 BC and re-used during the Roman occupation.

Waiting for the tide

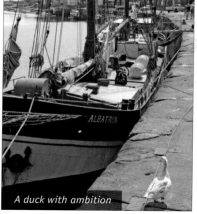
A duck with ambition

right, keep ahead on a narrower hedged way. It emerges at the edge of town beside a school, where you should follow the onward street down to the main road. Go a short distance to the left, crossing to a passageway between houses, which soon broadens into a back street, Plummers Hill. That in turn rises to The Buttlands, a long, spacious green around which the 19th-century gentry built their houses. At the top, go right and then left, dropping along Staithe Street, which leads back to the harbour.

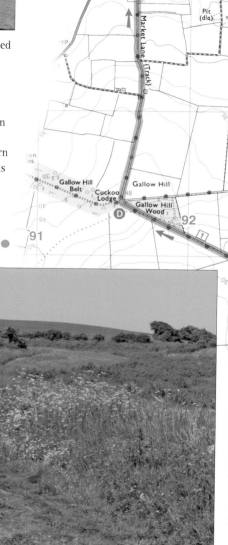
Beside the salt marshes

walk 24

The Weavers' Way to The Berney Arms

Start
Halvergate

Distance
9 miles (14.5km)

Height gain
Negligible

Approximate time
4 hours

Route terrain
Fenland tracks and field paths

Parking
Roadside parking in Halvergate

OS maps
Landranger 134 (Norwich & The Broads), Explorer OL40 (The Broads)

GPS waypoints

- TG 422 069
- Ⓐ TG 428 069
- Ⓑ TG 441 067
- Ⓒ TG 477 069
- Ⓓ TG 465 049
- Ⓔ TG 448 057
- Ⓕ TG 433 066

The Berney Arms is the most remote pub in Norfolk and, unless travelling by train or boat, the only way to it is on foot, for it stands in the middle of a vast marsh overlooking the confluence of the rivers Yare and Waveney. A shorter 5-mile walk utilises the train from Great Yarmouth Station, returning along the Weavers' Way beside Breydon Water. But to experience the full sense of its isolation, try this circular walk from the village of Halvergate on the edge of the fen.

Park near the **Red Lion** and follow Marsh Road out of Halvergate towards Great Yarmouth. Where it bends sharply left, leave the road along a broad track, signed as the Weavers'

Nesting beside The Fleet

Way **A**. It leads onto the reclaimed marsh, soon passing a small farmyard. Ignore a path later signed off right and continue ahead to Manor Farm **B**. Far to the north, traffic moves along the distant A47 to and from Great Yarmouth, which, apart from an occasional drainage pump, is the only feature to break this wide landscape.

The ongoing track winds on across the open fen, divided into irregular parcels of grazing by an intricate maze of ditches. The way follows The Fleet, a sluggish tributary of the Yare, eventually passing in succession two abandoned drainage mills, High's and Howard's. Farther on, Marsh Farm and Fleet Farm have only each other for company, the lonely way continuing

past both and through a gate to a crossing of tracks. Keep ahead, The Berney Arms and adjacent windmill now visible in the distance to the right, but still a goodly walk away. Reaching a concrete track, go right, soon meeting a level crossing that takes it over the railway line. Beyond, the path climbs past a pumping station onto the flood defence wall that bounds Breydon Water **C**.

At low tide, the River Yare shrinks to a narrow channel running within a huge expanse of mud-flat, which, particularly in winter, attracts pink-footed geese, teal, redshank and egret

SCALE 1:27777 or 2¼ INCHES to 1 MILE 3.6CM to 1KM

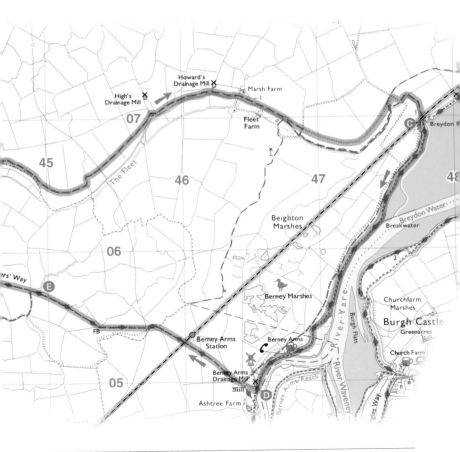

and where even spoonbill have been spotted. When the tide comes in, the water can lap the embankment and a line of green and red-topped stakes mark the safe channel for the passage of watercraft.

Walk to the right along the top of the wall, which protects the low-lying fields from inundation by the sea. It is still some 1¼ miles to The Berney Arms, the river steadily narrowing as you get closer. On the opposite bank is Burgh Castle, where, in the late 3rd century, the Romans built a garrison to help defend the coast against Saxon raiders.

The Berney Arms

The inn was originally a farmhouse, but has been a pub for the last century, a popular landing for those plying the river between Great Yarmouth and The Broads. It was eventually linked to the outside world when the railway, part of the county's first line, opened in 1844 between Great Yarmouth and Norwich. The Berney Arms is overlooked by the tallest windmill on the marshes, almost 70 feet high, and one of the few still retaining its working machinery. It was built around 1870 to grind clinker for the production of mortar and, when that trade died out, a large scoop wheel was erected beside it to lift water from the marshes, and it continued in use as a drainage mill until 1951. The area of marsh behind it is part of a nature reserve and dedicated to the memory of Michael Sago, one of Norfolk's leading ornithologists during the 20th century. Lapwing, wigeon, black-tailed godwit and curlew are commonly seen, with sparrowhawk and marsh harrier patrolling in search of a meal.

The ruins of the walls are just visible amongst the trees on the high ground overlooking the river. Approaching the confluence, the line of the dike and path moves back from the water's edge, skirting an area of reeds to rejoin the river at moorings in front of **The Berney Arms**.

At a Weavers' Way sign to Halvergate, just after passing the mill **D**, drop off the embankment and pass through a gate to join a track from cottages over to the left. As the track bends after crossing a ditch, bear off left past a telegraph post and through a gateway on a low ditch-flanked ridge. Keep ahead, passing through gates to a railway crossing beside the isolated Berney Arms Station.

Immediately beyond the railway crossing go through a gate on the right and walk left to a gated bridge. Continuing on the other bank, pass through a small gate, the ditch on your right and the church at Wickhampton ahead in the distance at the edge of the marsh. Reaching a gated field bridge, cross and bear left, now aiming for the faraway Mutton's Drainage Mill. Through a gate, keep parallel with a ditch now on your right, making for another gate beyond which is a grass track. Go left along that a short distance to a gate and stile on the right **E**.

Strike across the field to another gate, then aim just right of a marsh cottage sheltered by a small copse. Through a gate, turn right on a raised grass path to a stile 150 yds on. Cross the adjacent ditch and then turn right beside it. Close to the Mutton's Drainage Mill, but before reaching it, you are forced left by a channel. Go past a gate and follow another ditch to a gated bridge. Cross there and join the crest of a raised embankment to the left, eventually mounting a final stile and leaving the fields beside a cattle pen to rejoin the track along which the walk began **F**. Turn left back to Halvergate. ●

Reepham, Marriott's Way and Salle

Marriott's Way, a former railway branch line, is incorporated within this picturesque walk from Reepham, which also makes use of old greenways to visit the quite remarkable church at nearby Salle.

walk 25

Start
Reepham, from the church

Distance
9¾ miles (15.7km)

Height gain
245 feet (75m)

Approximate time
4½ hours

Route terrain
Field paths and old railway track, country lanes

Parking
Market place or town car park

OS maps
Landranger 133 (North East Norfolk), Explorer 238 (Dereham & Aylsham)

GPS waypoints
- TG 101 228
- Ⓐ TG 100 224
- Ⓑ TG 091 217
- Ⓒ TG 060 240
- Ⓓ TG 067 246
- Ⓔ TG 091 241
- Ⓕ TG 089 254
- Ⓖ TG 110 248

> **Reepham's churches** Wander into Reepham's churchyard and one is immediately struck by the fact that there are two churches actually joined together. More amazingly, there was also a third one here, All Saints', each serving separate parishes and having their own clergy. All Saints' was destroyed in a fire in 1543 and only a few ivy-covered stones remain. Whilst in many villages one of the churches has become redundant or derelict, Reepham has perhaps fared better than most and both surviving churches were 'restored' during the 19th century. St Michael's now serves as the parish hall while St Mary's continues in use for worship and has a fine mortuary monument of a 14th-century knight, Sir Roger de Kerdiston.

Leave the churchyard through a gate on the south side, walking right, along Church Street. Where it then bends into Back Street, turn left through an archway along an alley, Barn Lane. It heads out of town between abandoned meadows and a school, approaching a cottage beyond. Just before it Ⓐ, a waymarked path branches off right to meet a lane. Go right again and keep ahead over two sets of crossroads onto Broomhill Lane, which, just past another school, continues as a hedged path. It drops to a junction of tracks below the corner of the playing field. Turn left onto Back Lane and follow that for almost ½ mile. Approaching its end, bear right onto a narrow waymarked path, which climbs onto the embankment of the former railway Ⓑ.

To the right it runs towards Themelthorpe as a delightful path that alternates between low embankment and cutting. It has become well-wooded since the closure of the railway, but gaps in the trees offer glimpses across the pleasant undulating north Norfolk countryside. Cross a road where a bridge has been demolished and continue over two more bridges, eventually meeting another lane, Kerdiston Road, by a former crossing keeper's cottage Ⓒ.

The Themelthorpe Curve continues directly opposite, offering a short-cut back to Reepham along the Aylsham branch. To

Marriott's Way Two separate railways crossed near the keeper's cottage, the Norwich-Melton Constable line, built in 1882 and along which you have just walked, the other a link from the Great Eastern line near County School through Aylsham completed a year later. The line continued in use until the Lenwade concrete factory closed in 1985. The disused tracks now form part of Marriott's Way, named after William Marriott who was chief engineer for the Midland and Great Northern Joint Railway, which took over the Melton Constable line in 1893.

junction by the entrance to Kerdiston Manor **E**, turn left to Manor Farm. Keep forward where the metalling ends at a crossway between the farm and a cottage, subsequently bearing left at a fork to carry on along a field track. The way later narrows between hedges before breaking into a glade, Kerdy Green, the main trail winding ahead to continue at the edge of an open field. Walk on for a further 150 yds to a junction **F**.

Turn right on a broad farm road heading away between large fields towards the distant pinnacled tower of Salle Church. It wanders on for a mile

continue to Salle, however, take the lane left past the cottage, but then immediately turn off right to follow a track rising over a bridge that once spanned the Great Eastern line. The track meanders between high hedges whose boughs meet overhead to form a tunnel, eventually reaching a junction **D**.

Go right along another green track, which leads out to a junction of lanes. Take the one ahead, passing through the scattered hamlet of Kerdiston. At the next T-junction, head right towards Reepham, but when you reach another

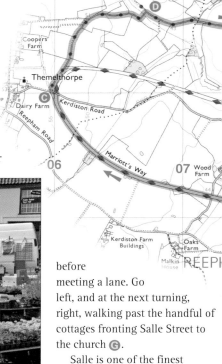

before meeting a lane. Go left, and at the next turning, right, walking past the handful of cottages fronting Salle Street to the church **G**.

Salle is one of the finest churches in Norfolk, its cathedral-like proportions and

Market day in Reepham

great architectural beauty funded by fortunes made in wool and the wealthy Trade Guilds.

Coming out of the church, go over the lane to the cricket field opposite. Bear left across, passing behind the village hall to the corner by a plantation of Scots pine. Pass through a gap into a field and go right along its edge, following the perimeter of the wood. Reaching the end of the long wind break, keep ahead on a cleared path through the crop, which emerges onto a lane at the far-right corner of the field. To the left, it leads to Reepham, shortly joined by the Marriott's Way from the right. Reaching a junction, go right, crossing the main road to then bear off left along Ollands Road past **The Crown Inn**, which takes you back to the centre of town.

SCALE 1:29412 or about 2⅛ INCHES to 1 MILE 3.4CM to 1KM

walk 26

Weeting Castle and Grime's Graves

Start
Santon Downham

Distance
10 miles (16.1km)

Height gain
180 feet (55m)

Approximate time
4½ hours

Route terrain
Riverside, field and forest tracks; short section along main road

Parking
Village car park

OS maps
Landranger 144 (Thetford & Diss), Explorer 229 (Thetford Forest in The Brecks)

GPS waypoints
TL 816 877
Ⓐ TL 817 878
Ⓑ TL 782 872
Ⓒ TL 776 885
Ⓓ TL 781 898
Ⓔ TL 797 897
Ⓕ TL 812 898
Ⓖ TL 811 894
Ⓗ TL 813 884

A truly delightful riverside walk, Norman castle and a prehistoric flint mine are just some of the features grabbing attention on this ramble through the Breckland forest surrounding Thetford. It begins from Santon Downham, a picturesque village that was all but obliterated by encroaching sand in the 17th century.

Leaving the car park, turn left along the lane towards Santon Warren. Immediately after crossing the Little Ouse River Ⓐ, drop to a path on the left and follow the bank downstream.

To the right is Little Ouse Meadow, an old mead occasionally inundated by the river. It is managed as traditional wetland grazing to benefit both plants and birds such as snipe and siskin. In fact, the whole valley between Thetford and Brandon is a designated nature reserve and encompasses a wide range of habitats.

The river cuts a lazy, sinuous course through the trees for almost 2½ miles until the outskirts of Brandon appear. The path then swings from the river behind a block of apartments onto a street, which in turn leads left to the main road. Turn right, soon passing over a level-crossing to a fork, where a minor road is signed to Weeting Ⓑ.

Take that, but immediately go left again into Fengate Drove. Beyond a small housing and light industrial estate it

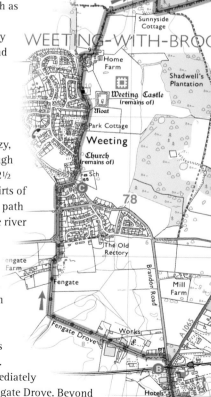

degrades to a track across a sandy heath. Later swinging right it passes Fengate Farm and in due course ends at a road junction. Walk forward with the main lane past houses, keeping ahead at a bend into a side street. That too soon becomes a track, which then curves right past a terrace of thatched cottages, reputedly the longest in the country, to emerge onto the main road .

Cross to the street opposite, which skirts a small housing estate. Keep with the perimeter road and then a rough track towards Weeting Castle, which can be glimpsed across the field. A path to it leaves just before the church.

The ongoing track winds past the church to Home Farm, where it dog-legs right and then left before continuing towards an isolated house. At a fork, bear right past its front and walk on to a junction at the edge of the forest **D**. Go right and, at the next corner, left, keeping at the edge of the trees. The wood eventually closes around the

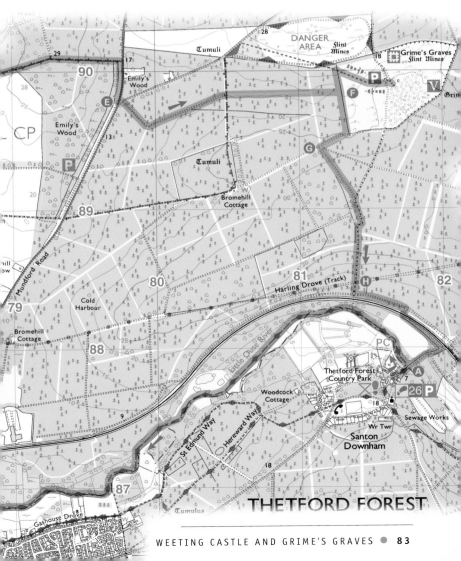

track, which ultimately ends at the main A1065. Turn right along the wide verge to a junction, where a lane leaves to Grime's Graves and West Tofts **E**.

Cross, but instead of following the lane, immediately turn off right past an earth barrier to find a faint path into the trees. Becoming more prominent, it runs for some 250 yds to a junction in a clearing. Go left along a broad, grass drove. After a little over ½ mile, at the second major crossing, continue forward on a narrower path that soon passes out of the trees. Keep ahead across grass to a path beside a fence delineating the perimeter of Grime's Graves **F**. To visit the site, where light refreshments are available, you should walk left to a stile and strike across the open grassland to the visitor centre. Be careful of your footing for the ground is very uneven and hides innumerable rabbit holes.

Return to the stile and retrace your steps beside the fence, continuing past the point at which you met it **F** to a gate and stile just beyond the corner of the English Heritage boundary. There, turn right along a broad grass swathe to a five-way junction beside a corrugated-roofed cistern **G**.

Take the second left off (a grass track, not the gravel track), initially following the edge of a felled area and ignoring side paths. Later encountering a crossing track, go right and then immediately left. Farther on, the trail curves right to meet another track. Follow that left, resuming your southerly direction. Eventually encountering a broad dirt road, Harling Drove **H**, keep ahead past barriers to a second track beside the railway and follow that left. Reaching a bridge, swing beneath it and continue on the other flank of the embankment to emerge onto a lane. Santon Downham is then a short walk to the right.

Strangers to Norfolk may be surprised to learn that sandstorms can occur. However those at Santon Downham between 1665 and 1670 were exceptional. Sand from a massive warren at Lakenheath began creeping towards the village and hundreds of acres of pasture and arable fields were engulfed. Despite the best efforts of the villagers to build barricades, some of the cottages were completely buried and even the river was partially blocked. ●

Castle Rising and Roydon Common

A substantial Norman castle nestling within an impressive monumental earthwork, a row of 17th-century almshouses and a rare heathland nature reserve are just some of the highlights to be seen on this longer circuit, which explores the gently rolling landscape overlooking Norfolk's north-west coastal plain.

walk 27

✎ Start
Castle Rising

✈ Distance
10½ miles (16.9km)

⛰ Height gain
230 feet (70m)

⏱ Approximate time
4½ hours

🐾 Route terrain
Field paths, tracks and country lanes

P Parking
Roadside parking in Castle Rising

OS maps
Landranger 132 (North West Norfolk), Explorer 250 (Norfolk Coast West)

📷 GPS waypoints
- ✎ TF 666 248
- Ⓐ TF 673 255
- Ⓑ TF 677 249
- Ⓒ TF 695 255
- Ⓓ TF 709 235
- Ⓔ TF 701 226
- Ⓕ TF 681 217
- Ⓖ TF 679 230
- Ⓗ TF 681 241

Castle Rising The drainage of the marshes from the 17th century onwards has completely changed the character of this section of Norfolk's coast. During the Middle Ages, Castle Rising was a busy port with boats navigating the Babingley River. The village's importance is emphasised by an imposing castle, built around 1138 by William de Albini. It was later home to Queen Isabella after the imprisonment and death of Edward II and extensively refurbished as a hunting lodge by her grandson, the Black Prince. The main hall still is hidden from outside view by a massive earthwork through which the gatehouse continues to provide the only entrance.

St Lawrence's Church, whose austere Victorian saddle-back roofed tower mimics that of the castle keep, is also worthy of exploration and contains the village's oldest stone artefact, a font. A relic from the original church demolished to make way for the castle, it carries an unusual carving of three cats' faces. This is possibly a reference to St Felix, who landed near here when he brought Christianity to East Anglia around AD 630.

📷 From a junction by the south-east corner of St Lawrence's Church and just up from **The Black Horse Inn**, walk along a narrow lane past the neat row of almshouses, Trinity

Roydon Common

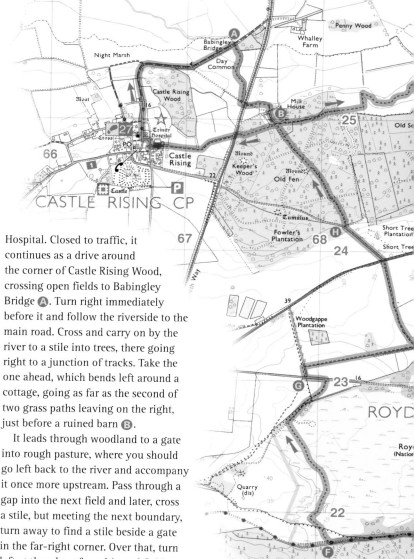

Hospital. Closed to traffic, it continues as a drive around the corner of Castle Rising Wood, crossing open fields to Babingley Bridge **A**. Turn right immediately before it and follow the riverside to the main road. Cross and carry on by the river to a stile into trees, there going right to a junction of tracks. Take the one ahead, which bends left around a cottage, going as far as the second of two grass paths leaving on the right, just before a ruined barn **B**.

It leads through woodland to a gate into rough pasture, where you should go left back to the river and accompany it once more upstream. Pass through a gap into the next field and later, cross a stile, but meeting the next boundary, turn away to find a stile beside a gate in the far-right corner. Over that, turn left at the edge of a cultivated field and walk out to a lane **C**.

Follow it right and, at the main road, go right again, leaving very soon along another lane signed left to Roydon. At the village boundary, turn left into St Andrews Lane, walking for a little more than ½ mile towards Congham. As the houses begin, look for a footpath signed through a break in the right-hand hedge **D**. If you reach the **Anvil Inn**, you have gone too far.

Strike across a crop field to a smaller pasture and veer right to a plank bridge, about halfway along the bottom edge. Pass through trees and continue across open paddock, leaving between houses at the far side in Roydon. Go right past the **Three Horse Shoes** and then a former garage, bearing left immediately after across a small green to a back lane. Continue right to a junction at the end **E**.

A kissing-gate opposite begins a broad, straight track at the edge of a wood. Keep going through occasional

Map labels:
Cross, Babingley R., C, White Hills Wood, White Hills, Gorse Moor, A149, 70, 12, 13, Moat Wood, 71, Oak Estate, D, Hall Farm, Willow Farm, Roydon, Lodge Farm, CP, P, E, Hudson's Fen, Millhill Common, Hill Farm, Mill Hill, Pott Row, Sch, Nook Farm, G

SCALE 1:27777 or 2¼ INCHES to 3.6 MILE 4CM to 1KM

| 0 | 200 | 400 | 600 | 800 METRES | 1 |
| 0 | 200 | 400 | 600 YARDS | ½ | KILOMETRES MILES |

gates and around a gentle bend, eventually joining another track from the right. The line of a former railway, it leads on through a final gate to a junction by a wooden cottage, Railway Gatehouse. Turn right and walk for ½ mile beside Roydon Common until you reach a gate on the right **F**. A signed footpath winds out across the open heath, skirting the base of a low sandy hill.

Eventually leaving the reserve, follow the ongoing track to the main road. Go left for 150 yds, crossing to a finger-posted gap in the hedge **G**. Briefly follow a break of Scots pine, then swing right along the boundary of a large field. Cresting the hill, join a farm track that passes through the hedge. Reaching a junction at the bottom, re-cross the boundary and head away north. Meeting the main road, cross to a lane opposite and walk on for ¼ mile to a stile beside a gate on the right **H**.

A clear path delves into a varied woodland, ending at the corner of a leylandii hedge near **B**. Turn left immediately before it to remain in the wood, now following a narrower path that soon cuts through to the main road. Cross to a gap opposite and continue between open fields. As the ground then begins to fall, keep forward with a hedge on your right, heading towards Castle Rising. Emerging between cottage gardens, follow the lane right back to the church. ●

Roydon Common Centuries of informal grazing have created this mosaic of bog and heathland habitats, a type of landscape that was once common in many parts of Britain. The land is now kept free of scrub by the Norfolk Wildlife Trust's 'flying flock' of hardy sheep and contains a surprising variety of plants from bog asphodel and cranberry to harebell and sheep's sorrel.

walk 28

Ringstead Downs and the Norfolk Coast

Start
Holme next the Sea

Distance
11 miles (17.8km)

Height gain
295 feet (90m)

Approximate time
5 hours

Route terrain
Field tracks and dunes, country lanes

Parking
Beach car park

Dog friendly
Dogs on lead along coastal reserve

OS maps
Landranger 132 (North West Norfolk), Explorer 250 (Norfolk Coast West)

GPS waypoints

🖉 TF 697 438
Ⓐ TF 685 429
Ⓑ TF 683 417
Ⓒ TF 686 399
Ⓓ TF 707 403
Ⓔ TF 726 404
Ⓕ TF 724 421
Ⓖ TF 722 444

Norfolk has a wealth of nature reserves. Coastal marshes, dunes, beach and chalk downs each display their individuality in a range of plant and animal species, while the views from the hilltops and dunes are superb.

🖉 Leaving the car park, head towards the coast, keeping a wary eye open for golfers driving off from a tee on the right as you cross a golf course. Pass through the dunes and turn left along the beach, which is striated with an endless succession of netted rock groynes to reduce coastal erosion. Ahead rises the low nose of St Edmund's Point at Hunstanton. After some ¾

The dunes approaching Gore Point

mile, and beyond a canted wartime pill-box, look for a wooden stake planted at the foot of the dunes that marks a path off the beach Ⓐ.

Dropping to a line of beach huts cowering behind the dunes, swing right between them and re-cross the links below the club house to a lane at the far side. A passageway facing you, colourfully dubbed 'Smugglers' Lane', leads between the houses, crossing a street and eventually ending at a junction of lanes. Bear right and walk out to the main road beside the Caley Hall Hotel. The lane opposite leads to a junction where ahead is St Mary's Church, overlooking the picturesque village pond. The present building dates to the beginning of the 14th century.

Return to the junction and turn left, climbing out of the village along Chapel Bank to a bend at the top of the hill Ⓑ.

There, strike off left onto a hedged track, which, as it later approaches a farm, skirts it to the left and then right to reach a junction. Go left to the next junction and turn right, the ongoing track falling gently between the fields in which the ruins of St Andrew's Chapel later appear to the right. Keep left with the track as it swings past a junction Ⓒ to pass Downs Farm, continuing beyond the buildings through two gates onto the Ringstead Downs Nature Reserve.

Centred on a long valley cut through chalk hills, Ringstead is a wonderful rolling grassland profuse in its flora. The open grassland is a managed landscape, the scrub kept at bay by the Norfolk Wildlife Trust's 'flying flock' of hardy sheep, an assortment of native breeds that munch their way through the Trust's various sites.

The path meanders on through occasional gates along the valley, eventually leaving the reserve on a track that emerges onto a lane. Ringstead lies to the left, the lane bending to a junction at the edge of the village Ⓓ. For refreshment, **The Gin Trap**, is a short distance to the left, but the onward route lies ahead, signed to Docking. At the next junction depart from the main lane, keeping ahead along Burnham Road. A long, straight drove, in time it leads past a small parking area on the edge of Courtyard Farm. Carry on along the lane for a further ¼ mile, looking for a waymarked track leaving over a cattle-grid on the left, opposite the entrance to the farmhouse Ⓔ. Immediately before a second cattle-grid, a gate on the left takes the path through a corner of a spinney. Joining a track go left and then right to climb at the field edge beside a belt of wood, a permissive path partway along taking you within the trees. At the top of the wood, turn right beside a hawthorn hedge studded with gnarled beech. At the far end, go left along a broad drove that crests the hill to end at a lane by a trig point **F**.

Keep going downhill along the lane opposite, crossing the main road at the bottom to another track beside a cottage almost facing you. Stay ahead where the track shortly bends, along a tree-lined grass path, swinging left and then right when you later reach a gate to continue through the last of the trees. The path again dog-legs over a bridged ditch onto the edge of the marsh grazing, following a drainage channel towards the still distant coast. At a crossing of paths the way swaps banks to put the ditch on your left and leads onto the sea defence embankment **G**.

Now on the Norfolk Coast Path, follow it left into the Holme Dunes NWT (Norfolk Wildlife Trust) Reserve, parts of which are not included within the general access area. To seaward lies Ragged Marsh, a remnant of the salt marsh that once extended inland to Holme village. Reaching the dunes a boarded path leads on beside an inland lagoon to the entrance of the Holme Bird Observatory at the edge of a pine wood. Permits are available to visit their hides, and you can help with bird ringing or join a guided walk.

Opposite the entrance, the onward path drops right and then left, continuing through the trees. The Holme Dunes visitor centre, run by the NWT, lies to the left, where drinks are available. The coast path, however, continues ahead onto the dunes. The sand has sometimes all but covered the boarded path, but keep to its line in order to reduce erosion damage.

After the salt marsh reappears, the path eventually reaches the golf course. Waymarks direct you around its seaward flank, before long returning you to the point at which you first gained the beach. Cut back to the car park, watching out for flying golf balls. ●

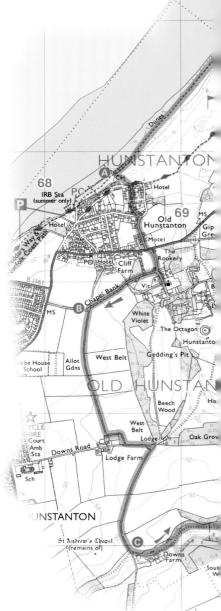

SCALE 1:27777 or 2¼ INCHES to 1 MILE 3.6CM to 1KM

0   200   400   600   800 METRES   1
                                    KILOMETRES
                                    MILES
0   200   400   600 YARDS   ½

West Sands

Mean High Water

45
Gore Point
Dunes
The Firs
Nature Reserve
Sluice
Broad Water
Firs Approach Road
Christie's Pool
Dunes
Hun Pool
G
5
FB
Flaxley
River Hun
Sprs
44
Plug Pits
PC
28 P
Home Farm
Caravan Park
Whitehall Farm
Holmbush
The Drove House
FB
Park
Littleholme
Seagate House
War Meml
Nursery
Holmhurst
8
A 149
Manor Farm
Holme next the Sea
43
A 149
Wayside
Field Barn
Main Way
Manor House
Long Plantation
70
Peddars Way & Norfolk Coast Path
71
Half Moon Plantation
72
Earthwork
Peddars Way
Green Bank
49
F
42
Ozonea
Broom Cover
Mill Farm
52
Field Barn
The Stratch
North Wood
CP
Green Broom Plantation
ark Ho
Earthwork
32
Bluestone Farm
41
Bluestone Farm Plantation
lf Moon ntation
Gedding's Farm
Ringstead Common
s Spring Meadow Pits
War Meml
P
Ringstead
PO
East End Farm
Burnham Road
1
E
Barn
Elms
Hall Farm
Ringstead Bury
16
Glebe Farm
Burnham Road Farm
RINGSTEAD CP
St Peter's Church (remains of)
Docking Road
New Wood
d Downs Reserve
Larch Plantation
40
Courtyard Farm

Further Information

 Walking Safety

Although the reasonably gentle countryside that is the subject of this book offers no real dangers to walkers at any time of the year, it is still advisable to take sensible precautions and follow certain well-tried guidelines.

Always take with you both warm and waterproof clothing and sufficient food and drink. Wear suitable footwear, such as strong walking boots or shoes that give a good grip over stony ground, on slippery slopes and in muddy conditions. Try to obtain a local weather forecast and bear it in mind before you start. Do not be afraid to abandon your proposed route and return to your starting point in the event of a sudden and unexpected deterioration in the weather.

All the walks described in this book will be safe to do, given due care and respect, even during the winter. Indeed, a crisp, fine winter day often provides perfect walking conditions, with firm ground underfoot and a clarity unique to this time of the year. The most difficult hazard likely to be encountered is mud, especially when walking along woodland and field paths, farm tracks and bridleways – the latter in particular can often get churned up by cyclists and horses. In summer, an additional difficulty may be narrow and overgrown paths, particularly along the edges of cultivated fields. Neither should constitute a major problem provided that the appropriate footwear is worn.

 The Ramblers

No organisation works more actively to protect and extend the rights and interests of walkers in the countryside than the Ramblers. Its aims are clear: to foster a greater knowledge, love and care of the countryside; to assist in the protection and enhancement of public rights of way and areas of natural beauty; to work for greater public access to the countryside; and to encourage more people to take up rambling as a healthy, recreational leisure activity.

It was founded in 1935 and since then the Ramblers has played a key role in preserving and developing the national footpath network, supporting the creation of national parks and encouraging the designation and waymarking of long-distance routes.

Our freedom of access to the countryside, now enshrined in legislation, is still in its early years and requires constant vigilance. But over and above this there will always be the problem of footpaths being illegally obstructed, disappearing through lack of use, or being extinguished by housing or road construction.

It is to meet such problems and dangers that the Ramblers exists and represents the interests of all walkers. The contact details for information on the Ramblers and how to become a member are given on page 95.

 Walkers and the Law

The Countryside and Rights of Way Act (CRoW Act 2000) extends the rights of access previously enjoyed by walkers in England and Wales. Implementation of these rights began on 19 September 2004. The Act amends existing legislation and for the first time provides access on foot to certain types of land – defined as mountain, moor, heath, down and registered common land.

Where You Can Go
Rights of Way
Prior to the introduction of the CRoW Act, walkers could only legally access the countryside along public rights of way. These are either 'footpaths' (for walkers only) or 'bridleways' (for walkers, riders on horseback and pedal cyclists). A third category called 'Byways open to all traffic'

(BOATs), is used by motorised vehicles as well as those using non-mechanised transport. Mainly they are green lanes, farm and estate roads, although occasionally they will be found crossing mountainous area.

Rights of way are marked on Ordnance Survey maps. Look for the green broken lines on the Explorer maps, or the red dashed lines on Landranger maps.

The term 'right of way' means exactly what it says. It gives a right of passage over what, for the most part, is private land. Under pre-CRoW legislation walkers were required to keep to the line of the right of way and not stray onto land on either side. If you did inadvertently wander off the right of way, either because of faulty map reading or because the route was not clearly indicated on the ground, you were technically trespassing.

Local authorities have a legal obligation to ensure that rights of way are kept clear and free of obstruction, and are signposted where they leave metalled roads. The duty of local authorities to install signposts extends to the placing of signs along a path or way, but only where the authority considers it necessary to have a signpost or waymark to assist persons unfamiliar with the locality.

The New Access Rights
Access Land
As well as being able to walk on existing rights of way, under the new legislation you now have access to large areas of open land. You can of course continue to use rights of way footpaths to cross this land, but the main difference is that you can now lawfully leave the path and wander at will, but only in areas designated as access land.

Where to Walk
Areas now covered by the new access rights – Access Land – are shown on Ordnance Survey Explorer maps bearing the access land symbol on the front cover.

'Access Land' is shown on Ordnance Survey maps by a light yellow tint surrounded by a pale orange border. New orange coloured 'i' symbols on the maps will show the location of permanent access information boards installed by the access authorities.

Restrictions
The right to walk on access land may lawfully be restricted by landowners, but whatever restrictions are put into place on access land they have no effect on existing rights of way, and you can continue to walk on them.

Dogs
Dogs can be taken on access land, but must be kept on leads of two metres or less between 1 March and 31 July, and at all times where they are near livestock. In addition landowners may impose a ban on all dogs from fields where lambing takes place for up to six weeks in any year. Dogs may be banned from moorland used for grouse shooting and breeding for up to five years.

General Obstructions
Obstructions can sometimes cause a problem on a walk and the most common of these is where the path across a field has been ploughed over. It is legal for a farmer to plough up a path provided that it is restored within two weeks. This does not always happen and you are faced with the dilemma of following the line of the path, even if this means treading on crops, or walking round the edge of the field. Although the latter course of action seems the most sensible, it does mean that you would be trespassing.

Other obstructions can vary from overhanging vegetation to wire fences across the path, locked gates or even a cattle feeder on the path.

Use common sense. If you can get round the obstruction without causing damage, do so. Otherwise only remove as much of the obstruction as is necessary to secure passage.

If the right of way is blocked and cannot be followed, there is a long-standing view that in such circumstances there is a right to deviate, but this cannot wholly be relied on. Although it is accepted in law that highways (and that includes rights of way) are for the public service, and if the usual track is impassable, it is for the general good that people should be entitled to pass into another line. However, this should not be taken as indicating a right to deviate whenever a way is impassable. If in doubt, retreat.

Report obstructions to the local authority and/or the Ramblers.

 ## Useful Organisations

The Broads Authority
Tel. 01603 610734
www.broads-authority.gov.uk

Broads Authority information centres:
Hoveton/Wroxham
Tel. 01603 782281 or 01603 756097
How Hill
Tel. 01603 756096 or 01692 678763
Whitlingham
Tel. 01603 756094 or 01603 617332

Camping and Caravanning Club
Site bookings Tel. 0845 130 7633
www.campingandcaravanningclub.co.uk

Campaign for National Parks
Tel. 020 7924 4077
www.cnp.org.uk

Campaign to Protect Rural England
Tel. 020 7981 2800
www.cpre.org.uk

Forestry Commission England
Tel. 01842 810271
www.forestry.gov.uk

Long Distance Walkers' Association
www.ldwa.org.uk

National Trust
Membership and general enquiries:
Tel. 0844 800 1895
www.nationaltrust.org.uk
East of England Regional Office:
Tel. 0128 474 7500

Natural England
Tel. 0300 060 6000
www.naturalengland.org.uk

Norfolk Coast Area of Outstanding Natural Beauty (AONB)
Tel. 01328 850530
www.norfolkcoastaonb.org.uk

Norfolk County Council
Bridleways and footpaths
Tel. 01603 222769
www.countrysideaccess.norfolk.gov.uk

Ramblers
Tel. 020 7339 8500
www.ramblers.org.uk

Tourist information:
East of England Tourism
Tel. 0333 3204 202
www.visiteastofengland.com

Youth Hostels Association
Tel. 0800 019 1700
Tel. 01629 592700
www.yha.org.uk

 ## Ordnance Survey Maps of Norfolk

The area of Norfolk is covered by Ordnance Survey 1:50 000 (1¼ inches to 1 mile or 2cm to 1km) scale Landranger map sheets 132, 133, 134, 143, 144 and 156. These all-purpose maps are packed with information to help you explore the area and show viewpoints, picnic sites, places of interest and caravan and camping sites.

To examine the Norfolk area in more detail and especially if you are planning walks, Ordnance Survey Explorer maps at 1:25 000 (2½ inches to 1 mile or 4cm to 1km) scale are ideal:

OL40 The Broads
228 March & Ely
229 Thetford Forest in The Brecks
230 Diss & Harleston
236 King's Lynn, Downham Market & Swaffham
237 Norwich
238 Dereham & Aylsham
250 Norfolk Coast West
251 Norfolk Coast Central
252 Norfolk Coast East

Text:	Dennis and Jan Kelsall,
Photography:	Dennis and Jan Kelsall
Editorial:	Ark Creative (UK) Ltd
Design:	Ark Creative (UK) Ltd

 This product includes mapping data licensed from Ordnance Survey® with the permission of the Controller of Her Majesty's Stationery Office. © Crown Copyright 2012. All rights reserved. Licence number 150002047. Ordnance Survey, the OS symbol and Pathfinder are registered trademarks and Explorer, Landranger and Outdoor Leisure are trademarks of the Ordnance Survey, the national mapping agency of Great Britain.

ISBN: 978-1-78059-044-8

While every care has been taken to ensure the accuracy of the route directions, the publishers cannot accept responsibility for errors or omissions, or for changes in details given. The countryside is not static: hedges and fences can be removed, stiles become gates, field boundaries can alter, footpaths can be rerouted and changes in ownership can result in the closure or diversion of some concessionary paths. Also, paths that are easy and pleasant for walking in fine conditions may become slippery, muddy and difficult in wet weather, while stepping stones across rivers and streams may become impassable.

If you find an inaccuracy in either the text or maps, please write to Crimson Publishing at the address below.

First published 2001 by Jarrold Publishing
Revised and reprinted 2004, 2007, 2010.

Printed in Singapore. 11/12

This edition first published in Great Britain 2012 by
Crimson Publishing,
Westminster House, Kew Road, Richmond, Surrey, TW9 2ND
www.crimsonpublishing.co.uk

Front cover: Berney Arms Mill beside the River Yare
Page 1: Beach huts at Holme next the Sea

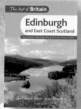